THE ILIAD -
TWENTY CENTURIES OF
TRANSLATION:
A CRITICAL VIEW

Michael M. Nikoletseas

ISBN: 9781469952109

Published in USA
Orders https://www.createspace.com/3777546

A catalog record of this book is available from the British Library
Shelfmark(s): General Reference Collection YD.2012.a.3134
UIN: BLL01016061795

Revised February 2013

Homer. Roman copy of a 5th century original

THE ILIAD-TWENTY CENTURIES OF TRANSLATION

ἀνέρες ἔστε φίλοι, μνήσασθε δὲ θούριδος ἀλκῆς,
ὄφρ᾽ ἂν ἐγὼν Ἀχιλῆος ἀμύμονος ἔντεα δύω
καλά, τὰ Πατρόκλοιο βίην ἐνάριξα κατακτάς.
Homer, The Iliad, 17.185-187

be men, my friends, think of war valor,
while I put on the armor of peerless Achilles,
the beautiful armor that I violently tore
from mighty Patroclus
when I conquered him.
Homer, The Iliad, 17.185-187
(Translation by Michael Nikoletseas)

CONTENTS

PREFACE

Matters of translation

The present book was not born, much like the Iliad, out of a concrete plan. It evolved over many years, lands, and stages of my personal search. It was only recently that the awareness crept up that in the pile of my fragmented notes, translations, poems, and treasured moments in poetry, there might be something worth communicating.

This book is off the traditional path of Homeric scholarship since I have not had the good fortune of spending my academic career with scholars of classics departments; instead, I earned my living in teaching and research in departments of natural science.

My passion for poetry has kept me captive to great men and women, some of which are: Homer, Sappho, Dickinson, Baudelaire, Whitman, Eliot, Pound, Faulkner, Seferis. The Iliad possessed me first as a war story, then as a fascinating treasure-cave of beautiful words and images, and lately as the arena on which the eternal male soul acts the drama that has been allotted to it.

My own poetry and prose has been enslaved by themes found in the Iliad. Having been given the gift of the Greek language as a native of Greece and as a student of the classics in Gymnasium more than half a century ago, my subsequent education and academic career in American universities places me in a privileged position; I have the luxury of diving in the ocean (πολυφλοίσβοιο θαλάσσης) of the Greek language at will and then emerging and drying up on the shores of English.

Homer has not been translated into English successfully, he will never be; he can only be paraphrased, and thus inspire

9

poets to create their own worlds. All the efforts by gifted poets and scholars so far have certainly contributed to our understanding of Homer; they have also contributed to the enrichment of English literature, but have not allowed anyone reading an English translation to experience Homer as Greek speakers can. Bentley said of Pope's translation: "It was a pretty poem, but must not be called Homer"[2].

Knowledge accruing while growing up in Greece, especially in the middle of the twentieth century when demotic Greek had not yet whitewashed Greek schools, seeing the world first in Homer's words, is not the same as the knowledge of Mathew Arnold's "φρόνιμος". Arnold's "Provost of Eton, or Professor Thompson at Cambridge, or Professor Jowett" in Oxford, awe inspiring as they may have been, could understand the words of Homer in relation to other words, and experience Homer through the images these words evoke, images of England and the English *zeitgeist*; they could not experience Homer as a Greek can. This thesis is not original with me; for example, Macpherson[1] in 1773 expressed similar views. However, Mathew Arnold (Arnold, M. 1960) has taken an antithetical position.

----

[1]Macpherson referring to the translations of the Iliad wrote: "These versions were rather paraphrases, than faithful translations: Attempts to give the spirit of Homer, without the character and peculiarities of his poetry and diction. Few succeeded even in the line, which they had avowedly chosen: And those, who have displayed the most animation, strength, and elegance, have left a regret, in the minds of many, that they have not been more attentive to the magnificent simplicity, if the epithet may be used, of an original, which can never be characteristically expressed in the antithetical quaintness of modern writing". (Macpherson, J., 1773).

The peculiarities of the Greek languages that have earned praise[1,2] are many, and have been meticulously studied.

In the list of positive characteristics, we may include the richness of vocabulary and concepts, and syntax. These have a powerful impact on the mind; they canalize perception and thought in directions that determine the overall power of a language in the arts as well as science. In addition to these elements, Greek possesses a musical sound. Bryant in his translation of the Iliad wrote:

"... grand and musical Greek to our less sonorous but still manly and flexible tongue".
(Bryant, W. C. 1870, p. iii).

Consider the first line of the Iliad:

μῆνιν ἄειδε θεὰ Πηληϊάδεω Ἀχιλῆος
meenin aeede thea Pele-eadeoo Achileeos

----

[1]"To attain to the nobility of Homer's manner may well be beyond the possibilities of modern English prose." Murray (1925, p. vii) in his introduction, dated as Athens, April 1923.

[2] Lucretius. *De Rerum Natura*, 1947.
Nec me animi fallit Graiorum obscura reperta
difficile inlustrare Latinis versibus esse,
multa novis verbis praesertim cum sit agendum
propter egestatem linguae et rerum novitatem;
Lucr. 1.136-140

 I know how hard it is in Latin verse
To tell the dark discoveries of the Greeks,
Chiefly because our pauper-speech must find
Strange terms to fit the strangeness of the thing; Lucr. 1.136-140

Let us push aside questions of meaning and imagery and concentrate on sound. Imagine that you do not know Greek at all and that you are present in a recitation of the Iliad in a festival. What will undoubtedly hit you is the music that the many long-drawn vowels create. Omitting the consonants, you would hear something like this:

ee,e,ha,ee,e,e,ha,ee,ee-e-a,e-oo,ha,i,ee-o

There are five words in this line, seventeen vowels (or diphthongs) out of which six are long drawn. What is striking is that on four occasions a vowel is succeeded by another vowel (ha-ee; e-ah; eee-ooo; eee-o), without the intervention of a consonant, and on one occasion three vowels are vocalized without the intervention of consonants (eee-e-a).

Now imagine that you do not know English at all and that you are listening to a recitation of the Iliad in English, e.g. the translation by Lattimore:

SING, goddess, the anger of Peleus' son Achilleus

You will hear the music produced by the vowels as follows:

e,o,e, e, a,e,o,e,e-ou,o,a,e,e-oo

There are eight words here, almost twice as many compared to the Greek; however, there are only fifteen vowels, out of which none is long drawn. Of the fifteen instances none contains a successive transition of vowel to another vowel; the only two such instances occur because of the presence of two Greek names (Peleus, Achilleus). These considerations and the ones I touch upon in the following paragraphs, delineate the space within which a translator stages his activities.

Towards a theory of translation

We find accounts that aim at the formulation of a theory of translation as early as the beginnings of Elizabethan reign (Amos, 1920). Another source of ideas regarding translation is to be found in the usually extensive prefaces of translations of the Iliad.

Macpherson, in his 1773 translation comments on the language and style of Homer: "Homer advances with apparent ease: Nor seems he ever to exert all his strength. He never deviates from his course, in search of ornament. He is not anxious about his language: Nor laborious in his versification. [...] He mixes the gravity of the historian with the dignity of the poet" (*The Iliad of Homer*, James Macpherson, London, 1773). A similar thesis is that of Matthew Arnold's need for "high truth" and "high seriousness" in poetry (*The Study of Poetry*, 1880, in *Essays in Criticism*, 1865, 1888). According to Arnold's criteria Homer, Dante and Shakespeare posses these virtues but Chaucer does not.

A more global caveat for translators is given by Morrice: "It has been said that the business of a translator is to enter so fully by attention and study into the mind of the original, that he may, as it were, look on every thing with the same eyes, and feel with the same soul" (Morrice, 1809).

Mathew Arnold argues that no one can tell us how Homer affected his audience. While there is truth in this, we have to consider that certain images, sounds, and other stimuli have a common impact, and this is phyletically determined. Arnold, as has already been mentioned, places the criterion with the knowledgeable scholar of Homer's works, which he claims would be distinguished professors at Cambridge or Oxford.

The criterion of staying close to the text has often been adopted. "I have endeavored to be strictly faithful in my rendering; to add nothing of my own, and to give the reader, so far as our language would allow, all that I found in the original." (The *Iliad of Homer*: translated into English blank verse by W. C. Bryant, Boston, 1870.)

Cowper has observed that Homer is the most perspicuous of poets; however, the problems faced by a translator whose language is not Greek are not eased by this fact. Similar views have been expressed by Bryant. "I have endeavored to preserve the simplicity of style which distinguishes the old Greek poet, who wrote for the popular ear and according to the genius of his language, and I have chosen such English as offers no violence to the ordinary usage and structure of our own". (*The Iliad of Homer*: translated into English blank verse by W. C. Bryant, Boston, 1870.)

It has been said that Homer's repetition of the epithets qualifying gods and heroes poses a problem in efforts to create translations of value. This is one of the indications that the feet of those translators may rest on wrong grounds. The Iliad and the Odyssey evolved as stories of brave men to be related to audiences. Anyone who has experienced the joy of listening to a tale knows the function repetition plays.

Considering the goals of this book, the account given in these paragraphs can only be sketchy and fragmentary, since the topic of theories of translation is vast and includes theories of art in general. For a systematic presentation of this issue, see the book by Flora Ross Amos (1920).

While these and many more considerations would certainly lead to better translations of the Iliad, there is one outstanding issue, the very foundation of all translations that permeates all others: The essence of the Iliad. What is the Iliad about? I will return to this question after we follow the history of the Iliad across the centuries, and after we critically evaluate fragments of translations of the Iliad.

THE ILIAD: ORIGINS

THE ILIAD-TWENTY CENTURIES OF TRANSLATION

THE ILIAD: ORIGINS

The title Ἰλιάς refers to the poem of the Trojan War, ἡ ποίησις Ἰλιάς, (genitive case Ἰλιάδος) "the Trojan poem". *Ilion* (Ἴλιον), in Latin *Ilium*, is Troy. Herodotus himself uses the term: "δῆλον δὲ κατὰ γὰρ ἐποίησε ἐν Ἰλιάδι" (*Hist.* 2.116).

The Iliad is the oldest work of literature in the western world. Scholars do not agree as to when it was written, however it is placed between the 11th and 7th centuries B.C. Herodotus placed Homer at approximately 400 years before him around 850 B.C. (Herodotus, *Book II, Euterpe*).

The Iliad evolved out of heroic poems (κλέα ανδρών). It is the prototype of *epic* poetry (ἔπος, από του επειν, ο εστί λέγειν, to say). The later definition of lyric or *melic* poetry and drama allowed for the distinction between the three forms of poetry. The word epic (επικός) was not used before Alexandrian times.

Epic poems were recited, not sung or acted. The very word "epos" in fact means "that which is said" as contrasted to that which is acted (ἔργω τε και ἔπει=in deed and in word. Cf. Plato, *Platonis De Legibus, Lib IX, 1823,* p. 282). Aristotle distinguishes epic poetry, εποποιία (he never used the term επικός), from drama, as narration and in meter mimicry (διηγηματική, καί εν μέτρω μιμητική, without acting, without πράττειν, (Aristotle, *Poet.* 13, 1966; also Jebb, R. C., 1894).

The Homeric works were originally propagated orally, as the Greek language did not posses a script. The Greek script was introduced ca. 800 B.C. as an adaptation of the Phoenician. Homeric Greek is the Greek language used by Homer in the Iliad and Odyssey; it is an archaic version of Ionic Greek, with influences from Aeolic Greek and other dialects.

Reference to writing is made in the tale of Bellerophon (*IL* 6.155–203). Wax tablets and skin scrolls were probably used in the mid-eighth century B.C. Herodotus mentions that goatskins were used to write on (Taylor, I., 1827).

Support for the proposition that the Iliad may have been written down around 700 B.C. comes from archeological findings. An inscription in Ischia in the Bay of Naples dating back to 740 B.C. may refer to a text of the Iliad. (Taplin, O., 2000, p. 32). The episode of Polyphemus in the Odyssey may be illustrated on Samos, Mykonos and Italy of 7th century B.C. (Pope, A., 2009)

Peisistratus (Πεισίστρατος) who lived ca 6th century B.C., made efforts in standardizing the Homeric works for use in the competitions of Panathenaia, however there is no evidence that a manuscript containing all of the text of the Iliad was produced.

Papyrus

Fragments of the Iliad have been preserved on papyri and parchment. In the period 1897-1907, excavations of the town-site of Oxyrhynchus in Egypt by B. P. Grenfell and A. S. Hunt (1908) recovered more than 100,000 pieces, fragments and scraps of papyrus, from the Roman and early Byzantine periods. Most of the papyri are written in Greek and have been deposited at the Bodleian Library of Oxford University. The text in early papyri may deviate from the standard text of Alexandrian scholars, a fact that has led to coining terms such as 'wild' or 'eccentric papyrus'.

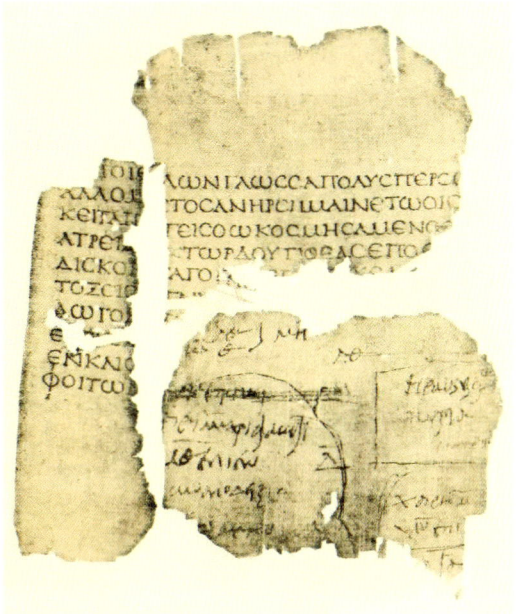

Papyrus Oxyrhynchus 20, second century. There are no stops, aspirates (breathings), or accents. *Iliad*, II, 804-

ΑΛΛΟΙ Δ ΑΛΛΩΝ ΓΛΩΣΣΑ ΠΟΛΥΣΠΕΡΕΩΝ ΑΝΘΡΩΠΩΝ
ΤΟΙΣΙΝ ΕΚΑΣΤΟΣ ΑΝΗΡ ΣΗΜΑΙΝΕΤΩ ΟΙΣΙ ΠΕΡ ΑΡΧΕΙ
ΤΩΝ Δ ΕΞΗΓΕΙΣΘΩ ΚΟΣΜΗΣΟΜΕΝΟΣ ΠΟΛΙΗΤΑΣ
ΩΣ ΕΦΑΘ ΕΚΤΩΡ Δ ΟΥ ΤΙ ΘΕΑΣ ΕΠΟΣ ΗΓΝΟΗΣΕΝ
ΑΙΨΑ Δ ΕΛΥΣ ΑΓΟΡΗΝ ΕΠΙ ΤΕΥΧΕΑ Δ ΕΣΣΕΥΟΝΤΟ
Iliad, 2.804-808

and different tongue of men of many seeds
these he should lead, having set in order the men of his city
so spoke Hector and he ignored not a word of the goddess
and immediately dismissed the assembly and they rushed to arms
Iliad, 2, 804-808
(Translated by M. Nikoletseas)

A papyrus roll may have been long enough to contain one book of the Iliad. Reading Greek and Latin papyri up to the middle ages is difficult because there is no word separation, and punctuation is rudimentary. Accentuation was introduced in Hellenistic times. The speech of a person was not precisely demarcated; the sign of : was usually placed before the speech of a god or person (Reynolds L. D. and N.G., Wilson, 1991).

In the third century B.C., different versions of the Iliad were studied and efforts for a standardized, "canonical" text were made. Zenodotus of Ephesus completed the first critical edition of Homer at the Library of Alexandria around 280 B.C.

The use of parchment led to the practice of creating separate leaves with writing on both sides (*codex*, plural *codices*) as early as the first century B.C. The Spanish-born epigrammatist and poet Martial who lived circa 40-104 A.D. writes:

Ilias et Priami regnis inimicus Ulixes
Multiplici pariter condita pelle latent
Mart. 14.148 (Martial. *M., 1925*)

Homer in a scroll codex
The Iliad and Ulysses enemy of Priam's kingdom
Together preserved in many folds of skin

The Greek text on which all modern versions are based, the ancient *vulgate*, was fixed in Alexandria during the second century B.C. by Aristarchus (Ἀρίσταρχος, probably 220–143 B.C.). He was the librarian of the library of Alexandria. Today he is considered the most influential of all scholars of Homeric poetry.

Aristarchus of Samothrace, detail from: *Apotheosis of Homer* (1827) by Jean Auguste Dominique Ingres (1780-1867). (Creative Commons, Wikipedia)

The Ambrosian Iliad

Ilias Ambrosiana (*Ilia picta*) is a manuscript on vellum (animal skin) thought to have been created in Constantinople between 493 and 508 A.D.

Achilles sacrificing to Zeus, *Ambrosian Iliad.* Milan, Biblioteca Ambrosiana, Cod. F. 205 Inf. These illustrations are unique, as we do not have any other illustration of the Iliad from ancient times.

Ambrosian Iliad, battle scenes

The Capture of Dolon. *Iliad* 10.338–381
Ambrosian Illiad
(Milan, Biblioteca Ambrosiana,
Cod. F. 205 Inf.) Picture XXXIV
(Wikimedia commons)

In late antiquity, the period of transition from Classical Antiquity to the Middle Ages (approximately between the second and eighth centuries A.D.), interest in the Homer's work dwindled. In Italy, interest in Homer began in the 15th century. By contrast, scholars continued studying Homer in the Eastern Roman Empire. We owe the revival of interest in the Iliad to Byzantine scholars who migrated to Italy.

Before the 5th century A.D., the Iliad circulated in manuscript form.

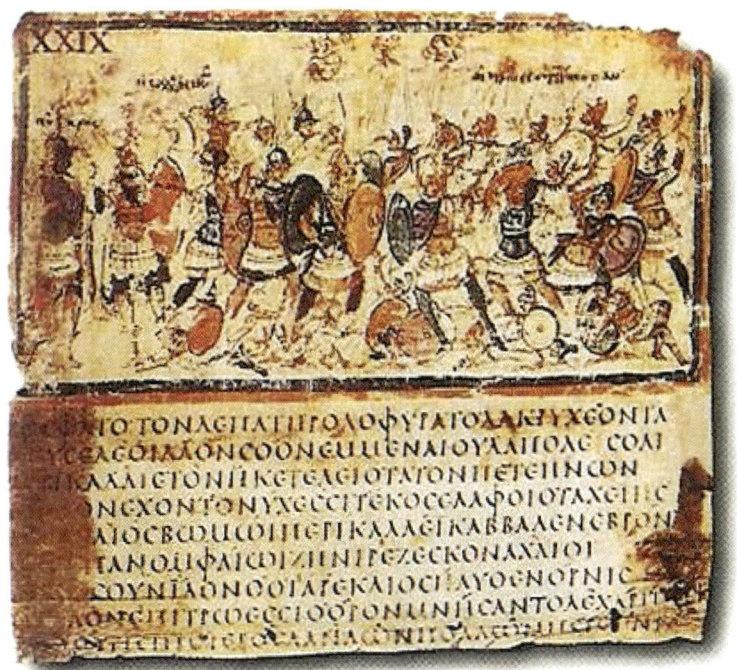

Iliad, Book 8, lines 245–53, Greek manuscript, late 5th, early 6th centuries A.D.
Milan, Biblioteca Ambrosiana, codex F205.
(Wikipedia Commons)

ὣς φάτο, τὸν δὲ πατὴρ ὀλοφύρατο δάκρυ χέοντα,
νεῦσε δέ οἱ λαὸν σόον ἔμμεναι οὐδ' ἀπολέσθαι.
αὐτίκα δ' αἰετὸν ἧκε τελειότατον πετεηνῶν,
νεβρὸν ἔχοντ' ὀνύχεσσι τέκος ἐλάφοιο ταχείης:
πὰρ δὲ Διὸς βωμῷ περικαλλέϊ κάββαλε νεβρόν,
ἔνθα πανομφαίῳ Ζηνὶ ῥέζεσκον Ἀχαιοί.
οἳ δ' ὡς οὖν εἴδονθ' ὅ τ' ἄρ' ἐκ Διὸς ἤλυθεν ὄρνις,
μᾶλλον ἐπὶ Τρώεσσι θόρον, μνήσαντο δὲ χάρμης.
ἔνθ' οὔ τις πρότερος Δαναῶν πολλῶν περ ἐόντων

IL. 8.245-253

So he spoke and the father pitied him as he was shedding tears
signaled assurance that his army would be safe and would not
perish.
and immediately he let go an eagle the most perfect of the
flying birds
a fawn having in his talons, born of swift deer
and on the side of Zeus' beautiful altar threw down the fawn,
where to Zeus of all ominous voices sacrificed the Achaeans
and as they really saw that obviously from Zeus came the bird,
the more on the Trojans leapt, and set their minds on the joy of
battle.
then no one foremost of the Danaans, and they were so many

IL. 8.245-253
(Translation by Michael Nikoletseas)

The Syriac palimpsest

Palimpsest is a term we find in Cicero. Romans and Greeks wrote on wax-coated tablets, which could be erased (by smoothening the surface) and used again. Palimpsest comes from the Greek words πάλιν = again, and ψάω = scrape. Palimpsest refers to parchment, sheets of animal hide. A palimpsest that contains the a 6th century Iliad (*Codex Nitriensis*) is kept in the British Museum.

Iliad, 24, 319-123. (Fragment of the Iliad from Cureton, W., 1851).

τόσς' ἄρα τοῦ ἑκάτερθεν ἔσαν πτερά· εἴσατο δέ σφι
δεξιὸς ἀΐξας ὑπὲρ ἄστεος· οἱ δὲ ἰδόντες
γήθησαν, καὶ πᾶσιν ἐνὶ φρεσὶ θυμὸς ἰάνθη.
Σπερχόμενος δ' ὃ γέρων ξεστοῦ ἐπεβήσετο δίφ[ρου],
ἐκ δ' ἔλασε προθύροιο καὶ αἰθούσης ἐριδούπου.
IL. 24.319-323

so wide on both sides were his wings; and it appeared to them a good omen, flying fast over the city; and when they saw him they rejoiced, and in the chest of all the heart warmed.
And in a hurry the old man stepped in the hewn chariot and away he drove from the gateway and the resounding portico.
IL. 24.319-323
(Translated by Michael Nikoletseas)

Compare the above fragment to the text in: Homer, *Homeri Opera in five volumes*. Oxford, Oxford University Press. 1920.

τόσσ᾽ ἄρα τοῦ ἑκάτερθεν ἔσαν πτερά: εἴσατο δέ σφι
δεξιὸς ἀΐξας διὰ ἄστεος: οἳ δὲ ἰδόντες
γήθησαν, καὶ πᾶσιν ἐνὶ φρεσὶ θυμὸς ἰάνθη.
σπερχόμενος δ᾽ ὃ γεραιὸς ἑοῦ ἐπεβήσετο δίφρου,
ἐκ δ᾽ ἔλασε προθύροιο καὶ αἰθούσης ἐριδούπου.
IL. 24.319-323

Venetus

Venetus A, is a tenth-century A.D. manuscript that contains the text of the Iliad as well as annotations, glosses, and commentaries, the "A scholia". Venetus A may be the work of Aristophanes of Byzantium of the Library of Alexandria. This is the oldest existing manuscript of Homer's Iliad. It is regarded as the best text of the Iliad. (Biblioteca Marciana in Venice as Codex Marcianus Graecus 454, now 822).

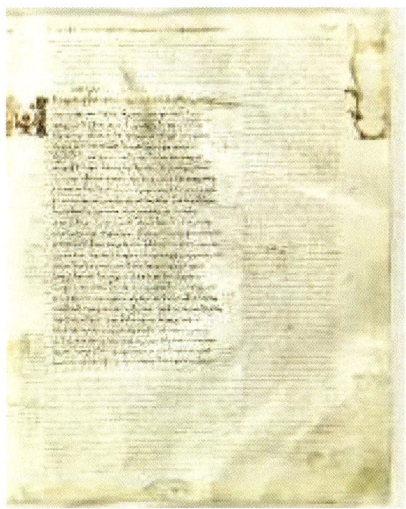

Venetus A, folio 12
(Center for Hellenic Studies of Harvard University).

Detail of top of previous image.
The first three lines of the Iliad:

μῆνιν ἄειδε θεὰ Πηληϊάδεω Ἀχιλῆος
οὐλομένην, ἣ μυρί᾽ Ἀχαιοῖς ἄλγε᾽ ἔθηκε,
πολλὰς δ᾽ ἰφθίμους ψυχὰς Ἄϊδι προΐαψεν
IL. 1.1-3

THE GREEK ILIAD

THE GREEK ILIAD

Homeric Greek

Opera. Demetrios Chalkokondyles, 1488
Ilias et Odyssea. J. Micyllus, 1541
Ilias. Ioannis Crespini Atrebatii, 1559
Ilias. Johann Guenther, 1563
Ilias. Georgius Bishop, 1591
Opera. Johannes Hays, 1679
Ilias. Thomas Day Seymour, 1695
Opera. Samuel Clarke, 1740
Works. Thomas Grenville, Richard Porson et al., 1800
Ilias et Odyssea. Richard Payne Knight, 1820
Works. Wilhelm Dindorf, 1828
Ilias. Dominicus Comparetti, 1901
Ilias et Odyssea. Eduardi Schwartz, 1924

Today, the Oxford edition by Munro and Allen is considered the standard text, the modern vulgate *(Homeri Opera*, D.B. Munro & T.W. Allen, Oxford University Press, first published in 1902).

The language in this text is "an artificial amalgamen of words, constructions and dialect-forms from different regions and different stages in the development of Greek from the late Bronze Age until around 700 BC". (Kirk, G. S., 1995).

The first printed publication (*editio princeps*) of the Iliad in Homeric Greek was that by Demetrios Chalkokondyles. It was published by Bernardus Nerlius, Nerius Nerlius, and Demetrius Damilas in Florence, Italy, in 1488.

Demetrios Chalkondyles (right). Fresco. Santa Maria Novella, Cappella Tornabuoni, Florence, Italy, 1486-1490. Artist Domenico Ghirlandaio: work: Zachariah in the Temple. (Demetrios Chalkokondyles, Demetrius Chalcocondyles in Latin; Greek: Δημήτριος Χαλκοκονδύλης; also found as Demetricocondyles, Chalcocondylas or Chalcondyles).

Bayerische Staatsbibliothek, München

Chalcocondyles (Δημήτριος Χαλκοκονδύλης)
Ὁμήρου τὰ σωζόμενα, Florence 1488

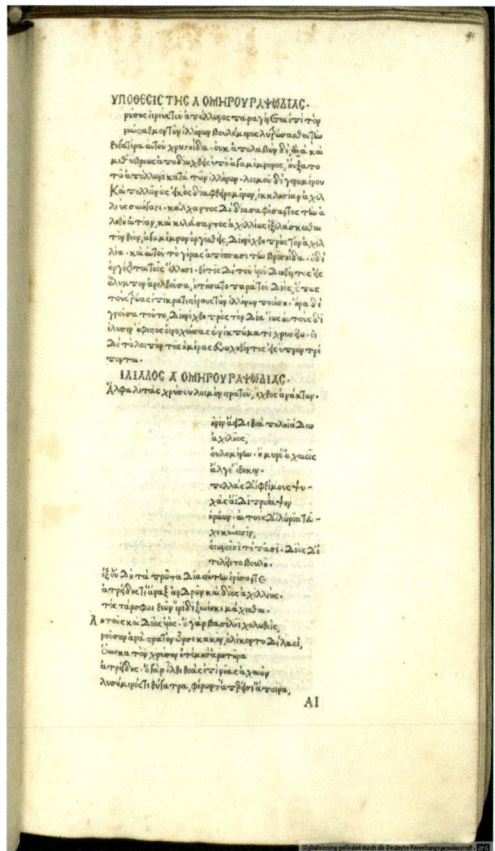

Bayerischen Staatsbibliothek

The first page of the first Iliad, *editio princeps,* by Chalcocondyles, 1488.
Homerus: Opera mit griech. Vita Homeri von Pseudo-Herodotus, Pseudo-
Plutarchus und Pseudo-Dion Chrysostomus. Mit Widmungsbrief an Piero
de' Medici, Florenz 13.1.1488, von Bernardus Nerlius, Florenz ,
1488.12.09. [vielm.: not before 1488/89.01.13.]

The first ten lines of the Iliad from the first edition by Chalcocondyles. The first letter M that occupied the vacant space on the left has not imaged.

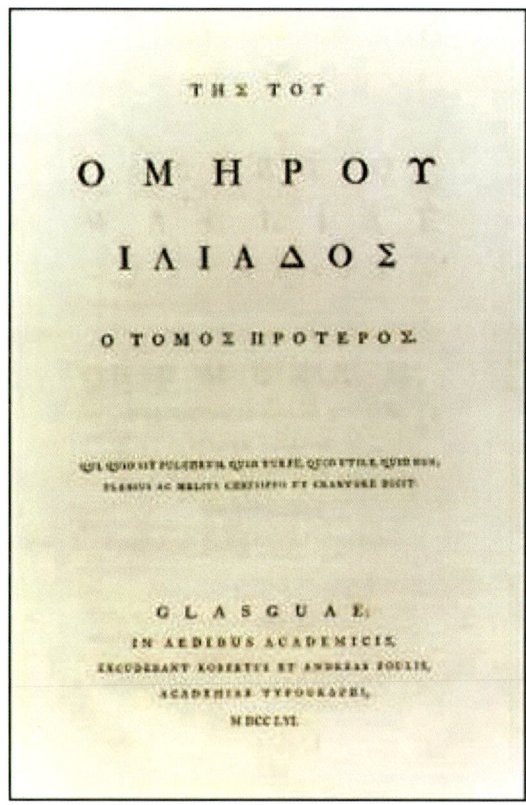

Edition in Greek, published by Andrew and Robert Foulis (1756-1758). The editors were the then James Moor, Professor of Greek, and George Muirhead, Professor of Latin, at the University of Glasgow.

Vernacular Greek

Archbishop Eustathius of Thessalonica

The work of Archbishop Eustathius of Thessalonica consists of commentaries on Homer's Iliad and Odyssey (Παρεκβολαὶ εἰς τὴν Ὁμήρου Ἰλιάδα καὶ Ὀδύσσειαν). It is a valuable source of commentaries from earlier scholars including grammarians of the library of Alexandria such as Aristarchus.

Eustathius. *Eustathii Commentarii Ad Homeri Iliadem*, Cambridge University Press, 2010. This is a re-edition of Johann Stallbaum (1793-1861) publication of Eustathii Commentarii ad Homeri Iliadem (1827-1830).

Nikolaos Loukanēs

The first important publication of Homer's Iliad in vernacular Greek (modern Greek, κοινή) was by Nikolaos Loukanēs in Venice in May of 1526. (Stampata in Venetia per Maestro Stefano da Sabio: il quale habita a Santo Maria Formosa: ad instantia di miser Damian di Santa Maria da Spici. M.D. XXVI nel mese di magio).

Την οργήν αδε καί λέγε ω θεά μου Καλλιόπη
Τοϋ Πηλείδου Ἀχιλλέως πώς έγένετ ολεθρία,
Καΐ πολλάς λύπας έποίσε εις τούς Ἀχαιούς δη πάντας,
Καί πολλάς ψυχάς ανδρείας πώς άπέστειλεν εις άδην,
Καί κυσί καί τοίς ορνέοις προς βοράν έδωκε τούτους-
Ὁ γαρ Ζεύς ήθελεν ουτως - άφ ου γουν φιλονεικουντες
Ἐχωρίσθησαν άλληλων ο,τε βασιλεύς Ἀτρείδης,
Και δ Ἀχιλλεύς ταχύπους. Τίς έκ τών θεών ω Μουσα,
Αίτιος υπήρχε τότε νά τούς βάλη εις τόσην μάχην;
Λέγε το του ποιητοϋ σου. Ἀπεκρίθ ή Καλλιόπη,
Κ' είπε πρός τόν ερωτώντα
Της Λητους παίς της ενδόξου, καί Διός του πανσεβάστου,
Ὁ Ἀπόλλων ο τοξότης. ούτος γαρ προς βασιλέα
Αγαμέμνονα Ἀτρείδην χολωθείς εν τη καρδία,
Ἐδιήγειρε την νόσον καί το στράτευμα φονεύει

IL. 1.1-10

Homērou Ilias metavlētheisa palai eis koinēn glōssam para Nik. Loukanou,
Homer, Nikolaos Loukanēs. Typ. A. Ktena kai S. Oikonomou, 1870

Rating

ούλομένην	+1	ολεθρία=disastrous, conveys idea of loss
προΐαψεν	-1	άπέστειλεν=sen t
ελώρια	-1	βοράν=food, prey
Overall	-1	

Note on ratings. I have identified three loci at which Homer paints subtle but dramatic images in the characteristic manner of his art. These loci are:

Line 2: ούλομένην (Il. 1.2)
Line 3: ελώρια (Il. 1.3)
Line 4: προΐαψεν (Il. 1.4)

Loukanes, Book 1: Apollo with his silver bow attacks the mules, dogs and then the men of the Greek army.

The translation by Loukanes is the first translation of the Iliad in a living language. The first French translation was published in 1530, the Italian in 1572, the English in 1581, the German in 1620, the Belgian in 1658, and the Spanish in 1788. Loukanes' Iliad is not a translation in the strict sense of the word but rather a paraphrasis. In addition, it is not complete since several lines of text have been omitted.

Other translations of the Iliad into Greek were those of Ioannis Tzetzes, Michail Psellos, Emanuel Chrysoloras, and Emanuel Moschopoulos.

Johannes Tzetzes (Ἰωάννης Τζέζης) was a Greek grammarian in Constantinople. His *Iliacus* (Ἰλιακά, 1793) consists of three poems: *Antehomerica* (Τά πρό Ὁμήρου), *Homerica* (τά Ὁμήρου, an abridgement of the Iliad) and *Posthomerica* (τά μεθ' Ὁμηρον). (Ioannis Tzetzae, *Antehomerica Homerica et Posthomerica,* Fridericus Iacobs, Lipsiae, 1793).

It should be noted that *Homerica* is not a translation of Homer's Iliad, it is rather a poem by Tzetze of the story related in the Iliad. Its merit lies in that extensive reference to other poets is made, a fact of considerable value.

Subsequent translations of the Iliad into Modern Greek were by Macedon Gerogios Rousiadis (1817-1818) and later by N. Argyriadis (1868).

Twentieth century translations of the Iliad into Modern Greek (δημοτική) are interesting as they range in scope from scholarship to sheer poetical showmanship. They are good tools in our understanding Homer's Iliad because they are the creation of native Greek speakers, a fact that has been overlooked in current scholarship. In spite of the fact that Modern Greek has been adulterated by many influences, there are still many words, proverbs, and demotic songs that clearly connect directly to Homeric times.

Niko Kazantzakis and I.Th. Kakridis.

Τη μάνητα, θεά, τραγουδά μας του ξακουστού Αχιλλέα,
ανάθεμα τη, πίκρες που 'δωκε στους Αχαιούς περίσσιες
και πλήθος αντρειωμένες έστειλε ψυχές στον Άδη κάτω
παλικαριών, στους σκύλους ρίχνοντας να φάνε τα κορμιά τους
και στα όρνια ολούθε —έτσι το θέλησε να γίνει τότε ο Δίας—
απ' τη στιγμή που πρωτοπιάστηκαν και χώρισαν οι δυο τους,
του Ατρέα ο γιος ο στρατοκράτορας κι ο μέγας Αχιλλέας.
Ποιος τάχα απ' τους θεούς τους έσπρωξε να μπούνε σ' έτοια
αμάχη;
Του Δία και της Λητώς τους έσπρωξεν ο γιος, που με το ρήγα
χολιάζοντας κακιά εξεσήκωσεν αρρώστια και πέθαιναν
στρατός πολύς
Il. 1.1-10
Ομήρου Ιλιάς. Μετάφραση: Ν. Καζαντζάκη & Ἰ. Θ. Κακριδῆ, Αθήνα 1955.
D. B. Monro and T. W. Allen. Oxford, 1920

Rating

ούλομένην	-1	Ανάθεμα= cursed
προΐαψεν	-1	έστειλε
ελώρια	-1	να φάνε =to eat
Overall	-3	

This pretentious, "theatrical" translation uses a Greek idiom that was never used in Greece except in the minds of scholars that looked westward. The emotionally charged style characteristic of most of Kazantzakis's work does not suit the sober language of Homer.

Iakovos Polylas

Ψάλλε θεά, τον τρομερό θυμόν του Αχιλλέως
Πώς έγινε στους Αχαιούς αρχή πολλών δακρύων.
Που ανδράγαθες ροβόλησε πολλές ψυχές στον Άδη
ηρώων, κι έδωκεν αυτούς αρπάγματα των σκύλων
και των ορνέων – και η βουλή γενόταν του Κρονίδη,
απ' ότ', εφιλονίκησαν κι εχωρισθήκαν πρώτα
ο Ατρείδης, άρχος των ανδρών, και ο θείος Αχιλλέας.
Κι απ'τους θεούς ποιός άναψε την έχθρα μεταξύ τους;
Ο Απόλλων, όπου οργίσθηκε του Ατρείδη βασιλέως
κι έφερε λώβαν στον στρατόν που εθέριζε τα πλήθη,

Il. 1.1-10 Ιάκωβος Πολυλάς, Ομήρου Ιλιάς, 1923

Rating

ούλομένην	-1	τρομερό=terrible
προΐαψεν	-1	ροβόλησε=sent
έλώρια	+1	Αρπάγματα= grabbings
Overall	-1	

This translation evokes memories of *demotic, kleftika* poems. Polylas stays close to the original text; however, his determination to be poetic leads him into inaccuracies.

Polylas "revealed a conscientious tendency toward archaic grandeur. His translation at no time captivates us, but it very often inspires an admiration and a feeling of respect close to those which a reading of the original inspires". (Dēmaras, K. 1972, p. 298).

Alexander Pallis

Μούσα, τραγουδά το θυμό του ξακουστού Αχιλέα,
τον έρμο ! π' όλους πότισε τους Αχαιούς φαρμάκια,
και πλήθος έστειλε ψυχές λεβέντικες στον Άδη
οπλαρχηγώνε, κι' έθρεψε με τα κορμιά τους σκύλους
κι' όλα τα όρνια (του Διός έτσι είχε η γνώμη ορίσει),
απ' την αρχή σαν πιάστηκε με το γοργό Αχιλλέα
τ' Ατρέα ο πρωταφέντης γιος και χώρισαν οι διό τους.
Πιός τάχα λες τους έσπρωξε θεός να λογοφέρουν;
Του Δία ο γιος και της Λητός, που με τον Αγαμέμνο
θύμωσε κι' έρηξε κακή μες στο στρατό πανούκλα,
και κόσμος πέθαινε

Il. 1.1-10 Αλέξανδρος Πάλλης, Η Ιλιάδα,1904

Rating

ούλομένην	-1	έρμο=correct, but misapplied to Achilles
προΐαψεν	-1	έστειλε=sent
ἐλώρια	-1	έθρεψε=fed
Overall	-3	

The influence of Homer on Byzantine and Modern Greek literature cannot be overlooked. "A phrase in Homer can be enough to create an obsession." (Bruce Merry, B., 2004, p. 179).

Seferis's poem *Eleni* is based the idea of Helen being a shadow in Troy. His poem *The King of Asine*, is built on a phrase in the Iliad (IL. 2, 560), "Hermione and Asine" two cities on the Peloponnese.

Elytis sees his work as "my poor house on the sandy shores of Homer", a claim that can be supported with difficulty, given the abstract-surrealistic and introspective nature of his work. Elytis's work should be viewed as the antipode of Homer's. Homer is objective, restrained, laconic, while Elytis thrives in verbiage, excess of emotion and introspection. I believe what Elytis means in the above quotation is his love of the Greek language.

Kavafi owned a copy of the 1904 edition of the Iliad by Pallis. Kavafi wrote poems on Homeric themes, some of which are *Ithaca, Trojans, The horses of Achilles, Priam's nocturnal journey,* and others. One could say that all of his poetry deals with *klea andron*, though apparently not epic. Oddly enough, there are common principles in the two poets, for example in Kavafi's homoeroticism the preoccupation of his heroes is the same as that of the heroes of Homer: the constant measuring up of male-to-male, the adoration of male virtues.

M. Nikoletseas' book *Rape in Ahmetaga* (2011), inspired by the speech of Hector over the naked body of Patroclus, is a psychoanalytic, anthropological look into male *rites de passage, mana*, aggression, and rituals.

THE LATIN ILIAD

THE LATIN ILIAD

The Latin translations of Homer's Iliad are important for the critical evaluation of English translations because of the temporal proximity of the two languages. Additionally we know that early English translators relied on Latin translations because their knowledge of Greek was not, in some cases, adequate.

Ilias Latina

Publius Baebius Italicus, a Roman Senator, is credited with the following Latin translation of the Iliad in the decade 60 A.D. - 70 A.D. The work is known as *Homerus Latinus* and was formerly attributed to Pindarus Thebaeus. The following is from an edition of 1885.

Iram pande mihi Pelidae, Diva, superbi
Tristia quae miseris injecit funera Grais
Atque animas fortes heroum tradidit orco,
Latrantumque dedit rostris volucrumque trahendos
Ipsorum exsangues, inhumatis ossibus artus.
Confiebat enim summi sententia regis,
volverunt ex quo discordi pectora turbos,
Sceptriger Atrides et bello clarus Achilles.
Quis deus hos jussit ira contendere tristi?
Latonae et magni proles Jovis. Ille Pelasgum
infestus regi pestem in praecordia misit
Implicuitque gravi Danaorum corpora morbo.
Il. 1.1-10

Note: line 4: Latrantumque dedit rostris volucrumque
trahendos

Rating

οὐλομένην	-1	Tristia
προΐαψεν	-1	tradidit=sent, delivered
ἐλώρια	+1	trahendos=traho, to drag along
Overall	-1	

μῆνιν ἄειδε θεὰ Πηληϊάδεω Ἀχιλῆος
οὐλομένην, ἣ μυρί᾽ Ἀχαιοῖς ἄλγε᾽ ἔθηκε,
πολλὰς δ᾽ ἰφθίμους ψυχὰς Ἄϊδι προΐαψεν
ἡρώων, αὐτοὺς δὲ ἐλώρια τεῦχε κύνεσσιν
οἰωνοῖσί τε πᾶσι, Διὸς δ᾽ ἐτελείετο βουλή,
ἐξ οὗ δὴ τὰ πρῶτα διαστήτην ἐρίσαντε
Ἀτρεΐδης τε ἄναξ ἀνδρῶν καὶ δῖος Ἀχιλλεύς.
τίς τ᾽ ἄρ σφωε θεῶν ἔριδι ξυνέηκε μάχεσθαι;
Λητοῦς καὶ Διὸς υἱός: ὃ γὰρ βασιλῆϊ χολωθεὶς
νοῦσον ἀνὰ στρατὸν ὄρσε κακήν, ὀλέκοντο δὲ λαοί,
Il. 1.1-10

Nunc iram Aeacidae tristem miseramque futuram
Diva cane et quantos Grais dedit ille dolores
Quotque animas fortes heroum miserit Orcho
Quantaque tum canibus miserorum corpora passim
Atque avibus lanianda tulit, quo tempore primum
Atrides, rector populorum et dius Achilles
Inter se certant, sic Iupiter ipse volebat.
Quis deus hic tantos irarum miscuit aestus?
Latonae genitus, contempto numine saevo
Infensus regi, pestem conciverat atram
Castra per et populum procumbunt undique morbo.
IL. 1.1-10

Marsuppini, Carlo Arezzo 1399 - Firenze 1453, liber primus Homeri, liber primus Homeri Iliad. liber primus Homeri (M. Lehnerdt, 1907)

Rating

οὐλομένην	-1	tristem=sad
προΐαψεν	-1	miserit=sent
ἑλώρια	+1	trahendos=traho, to drag along
Overall	-1	

Iram cane, dea, Pelidae Achillis pernìciosam,
quae plurima Achiuis mala attulit; multasque
fortes animas orco demisit heroum, ipsosque
praedam fecit canibus, alitibusque quibusuis:
Iouis autem perficiebatur consilium: ex quo vti-
que primum dissederunt litigando Atridesque,
rex virorum, et nobilis Achilles.

    Quisnam igitur eos deorum contentione com-
mifit vt pugnarent? Latonae et Iouis filius: hic
enim régi iratus luem per exercitum excitauit
pestiferam; peribant autem copiae
Il. 1.1-10

Homeri Carmina cum brevi annotatione: Versio latina Iliadis
By Homer, Curante C. G. Heyne, Lipsiae, in libraria Weidmannia, 1802

Rating

οὐλομένην	-1	pernìciosam
προΐαψεν	+1	demisit=cast down, throw, thrust, plunge
ἑλώρια	-1	praedam=prey
Overall	-1	

μῆνιν ἄειδε θεὰ Πηληϊάδεω Ἀχιλῆος
οὐλομένην, ἣ μυρί᾽ Ἀχαιοῖς ἄλγε᾽ ἔθηκε,

IRAM cane, Dea, Pelidae Achillis
Perniciosam, quae plurimos Achivis dolores fecit;

Πολλάς δ' ιφθίμους ψυχάς άιδὶ προίαψεν
Ἡρώων, αύτούς δ' ελώρια τεύχε κύνεσσιν,
Οιωνοίσί τε πάσι (Διός δ' ετελείετο βουλή)
ἐξ ού δή τά πρῶτα διαστήτην ερίσαντε
Ατρείδης τε, άναξ ανδρών, καί δίος Αχιλλεύς.

Multasque fortes animas orco praemature misit
Heroum, ipsosque praedam-discerpendam fecit canibus,
Alitibusque omnibus: Jovis autem perficiebatur consilium:
Ex quo utique primum disjuncti sunt litigantes
Atridesque, rex virorum, et nobilis Achiles.

Τίς τ' άρ σφώς θεών έριδι ξυνέηκε μάχεσθαι;
Λητούς & Διός υιός' ο γάρ βασιλήι χολωθείς
Νούσον ανά στρατόν ὦρσε κακήν᾽ ολέκοντο δε λαοί

Et quisnam igitur eos Deorum, contentione commisit, ut pugnarent?
Latona et Jovis filius: Hic enim regi iratus
Morbum per exercitum excitavit pestiferum : peribant autem populi:
IL. 1.1-10

Ilias, graece et latine. Ex recensione et cum notis Samuelis Clarke.
Nova ed. Published 1845 by R. Martin in Edinburgi . Written in Latin.

Rating

οὐλομένην	-1	Perniciosam
προΐαψεν	-1	praemature misit=prematurely sent
ἑλώρια	+1	discerpendam, discerpo=tear to pieces
Overall	-1	

55

THE ENGLISH ILIAD

"A great age of literature is perhaps always a great age of translations; or follows it" (LE, 1916, 232).
Ezra Pound

THE ENGLISH ILIAD

The earliest English translations were based on French (the translation of Arthur Hall) or Latin texts (the translation of Chapman) rather than Homeric Greek.

The Iliad, a list of English translations

Ten Books of Homers Iliades, Translated Out of French, by Arthur Hall Esquire,1581
The Whole Works of Homer. George Chapman, 1612
Iliad. John Ogilby, 1660
The Iliad and Odyssey of Homer. Thomas Hobbes, 1673
The Iliad of Homer. Alexander Pope, William Broome, and Elijah Fenton, 1726
The Iliad of Homer. James Macpherson, 1773
The Iliad and Odyssey of Homer. William Cowper, 1791
The Iliad of Homer rendered into English blank verse. Earl of Derby, 1867
The Iliad of Homer. William Cullen Bryant, 1870
Iliad. Andrew Land, Walter Leaf, and Ernest Myers, 1883
The Iliad of Homer. Samuel Butler, 1898
Iliad. A. T. Murray, 1924
Iliad. W.H.D. Rouse, 1937
Iliad. Richmond Lattimore, 1951
Iliad. Robert Fitzgerald. 1974
The Iliad. Martin Hammond, 1987
The Iliad. Robert Fagles, 1990
The Iliad. Ennis Rees, 1991
The Iliad. Michael Pierce Reck, 1994
The Iliad. Stanley Lombardo, 1997

HALL

The first English translation of the Iliad was by Arthur Hall in 1581. Hall based his translation on the French translation by Hugues Salel of 1555 and not on the Homeric text.

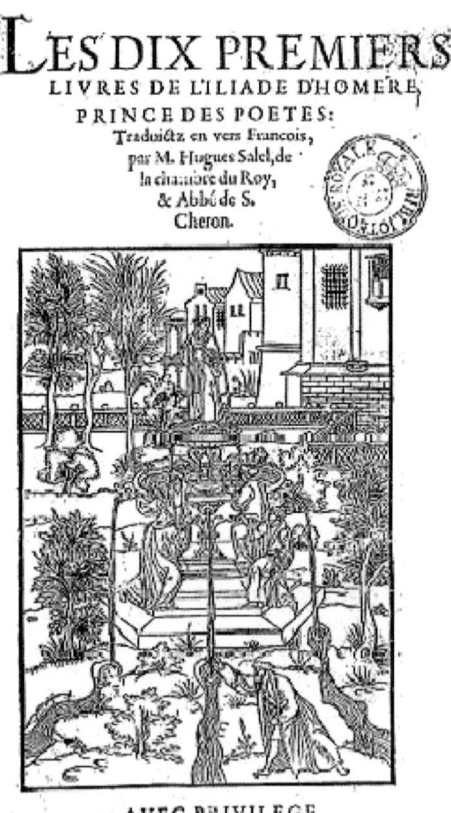

Les dix premiers LIVRES DE L'ILIADE D'HOMERE,
PRINCE DES POETES : Traduictz en vers Francois,
par M. Hugues Salel, de la chambre du Roy,
& Abbé de S.
Cheron.

JE TE Supply Deeſſe Gracieuſe,
Vouloir chanter l'Ire pernicieuſe,
Dont Achillés fut tellement eſpris,
Que par icelle, un grãd nombre d'eſpritz

Des princes Grecs, par dangereux encombres,
Feit lors deſcente aux infernales vmbres :
Et leurs beaulx Corps, priuez de ſepulture,
Furent aux chiens, & aux oiſeaulx paſture.
Certainement c'eſtoit la volunté
De Iuppiter, grandement irrité :
Des qu'il cogneut Agamemnon contendre
Contre Achillés, & ſur luy entreprendre.
Enſeigne moy, qui fut celuy des Dieux,
Qui leur cauſa debat tant odieux ?

　　Ce fut Phœbus, le clair Filz de Latone,
Et du grand Dieu qui Greſle, Eſclaire, & Tone.
Lequel eſtant griefuement courroucé
D'Agamemnon, qui auoit repoulſe
Chryſes ſon Prebſtre, vſant de violence,
Soudain tranſmiſt mortele peſtilence
En l'oſt des Grecs : dont grand malheur ſuruint.

*Les dix premiers LIVRES DE L'ILIADE D'HOMERE,
PRINCE DES POETES* : Traduictz en vers Francois,
par M. Hugues Salel, de la chambre du Roy, & Abbé de S.
Cheron

Rating

οὐλομένην	-1	pernicieuſe
προΐαψεν	-1	Feit lors deſcente
ἑλώρια	-1	pâture =food
Overall	-3	

Arthur Hall, 1581

I Thee beseech, O Goddesse milde, the hatefull hate to plaine,
Whereby Achilles was so wroong, and grewe in suche disdaine,
That thousandes of the Greekish Dukes, in hard and heauie plight,
To Plutoes Courte did yeelde their soules, and gaping lay vpright,
Those sencelesse trunckes of buriall voide, by them erst gaily borne,
By rauening curres, and carreine foules, in peeces to be torne.
Gainst Agamemn of Ioue his wrath, so kindled was the fire,
That he Achil to deere, and crosse so deepely did conspire.
O Lady shew what God beganne this hateful quarrell thus,
It was the heire of Latona, the gallant gay Phoebus,
Who had to sire that mighty God, who down his lightning throws,
With stormes of haile, and thunderclaps: the God in choller grows,
That Agamemn roughly a suite his Chryses Priest refusd,
In Greekish cap his plages he flings, their state which gretly brusd.

Ten books of Homers Iliades, translated out of French, by Arthur
Hall Esquire. At London: Imprinted by Henry Bynneman? for] Ralph Nevvberie,
1581.

μῆνιν ἄειδε θεὰ Πηληϊάδεω Ἀχιλῆος
οὐλομένην, ἣ μυρί᾽ Ἀχαιοῖς ἄλγε᾽ ἔθηκε,
πολλὰς δ᾽ ἰφθίμους ψυχὰς Ἄϊδι προΐαψεν
ἡρώων, αὐτοὺς δὲ ἑλώρια τεῦχε κύνεσσιν
5οἰωνοῖσί τε πᾶσι, Διὸς δ᾽ ἐτελείετο βουλή,
ἐξ οὗ δὴ τὰ πρῶτα διαστήτην ἐρίσαντε
Ἀτρεΐδης τε ἄναξ ἀνδρῶν καὶ δῖος Ἀχιλλεύς.
τίς τ᾽ ἄρ σφωε θεῶν ἔριδι ξυνέηκε μάχεσθαι;
Λητοῦς καὶ Διὸς υἱός: ὃ γὰρ βασιλῆϊ χολωθεὶς
10νοῦσον ἀνὰ στρατὸν ὄρσε κακήν, ὀλέκοντο δὲ λαοί

Rating

οὐλομένην	-1	hatefull
προΐαψεν	-1	yeelde
ἑλώρια	+1	in peeces to be torne
Overall	-1	

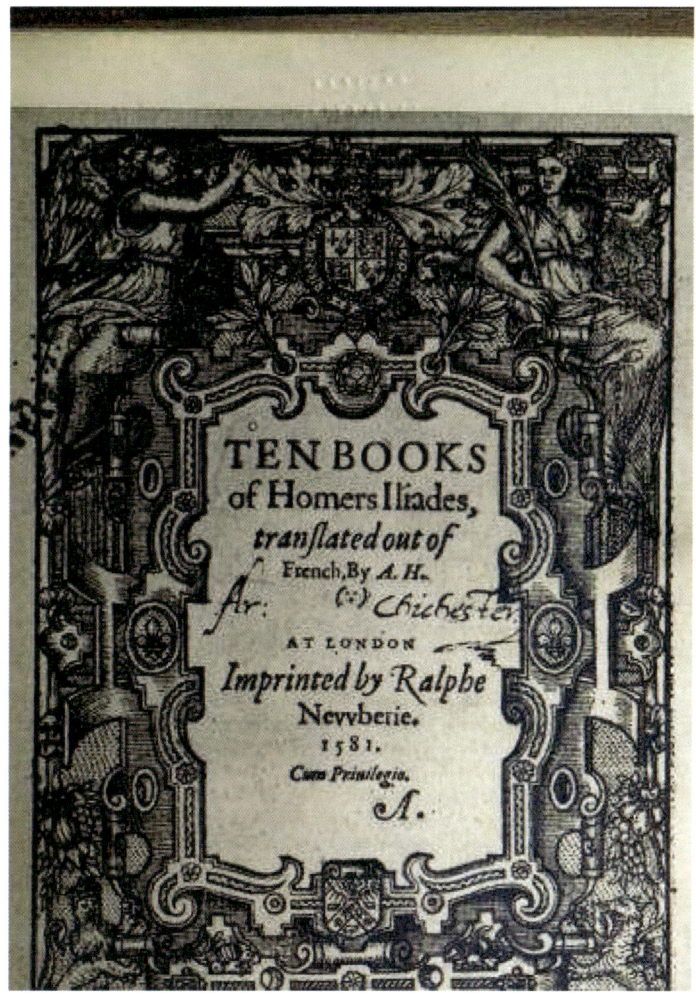

Arthur Hall, cover of the 1581 edition of the Iliad

CHAPMAN

George Chapman's translation of the Iliad (1612) was based on the French edition by Jean de Sponde, alias Io, Spondani (Basle, 1583) in which de Sponde wrote the commentary of a Latin translation with parallel Greek text by Andreas Divus. It should be noted that the Divus book was not the original but a subsequent edition in which alterations had been effected.

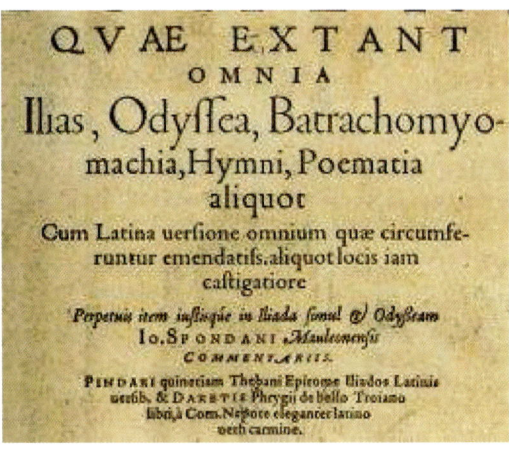

Homeri quae extant omnia
Homerus, Jean de Sponde
Evs. Episcopii opera, 1603

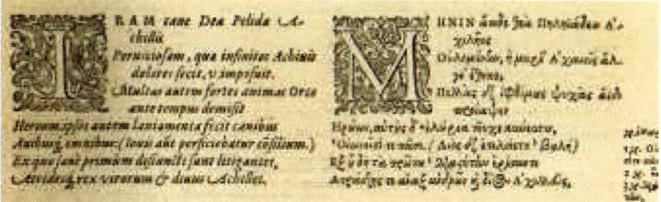

The first page of de Sponde's edition of the Iliad (IL. I, 1-10)

Iram cane, Dea Pelidae Achillis
Perniciosam, quae infinitos Achivis dolores fecit,v.imposuit
Multas autem fortes animas orco antetempus demisit
Heroum.ipsos autem laniamenta fecit canibus
Avibusque omnibus: Jovis aut perficiebatur consilium,
Ex quo sane primum disiuncti sunt litigantes,
Atridesque, rex virorum, et diuus Achilles.
Quisnam ipsos Deorum liti commisit ut pugnarent?
Latonae et Jovis filius. hic enim? regi iratus
Morbum per exercitum excitavit malu, peribant autem populi

The first page of de Sponde's edition of the Iliad, Latin text. (IL. I.1-10)

Rating

οὐλομένην	-1	Perniciosam
προΐαψεν	+1	antetempus demisit=prematurely cast down, throw, thrust, plunge
ἐλώρια	+1	laniamenta=torn to pieces
Overall	+1	

CHAPMAN

ACHILLES' baneful wrath resound, O Goddess, that impos'd
Infinite sorrows on the Greeks, and many bravo souls los'd
From breasts heroic; sent them far to that invisible cave
That no light comforts; and their limbs to dogs and
vultures gave:
What god gave Eris their command, and op'd that fighting
vein?
Jove's and Latona's son; who fir'd against the king of men,
For contumely shown his priest, infectious sickness sent
To plague the army, and to death by troops the soldiers went

George Chapman, *The Iliads of Homer*, Prince of Poets, London, 1865

Rating

οὐλομένην	-1	baneful
προΐαψεν	-1	sent far
ἑλώρια	-1	gave
Overall	-3	

μῆνιν ἄειδε θεὰ Πηληϊάδεω Ἀχιλῆος
οὐλομένην, ἣ μυρί᾽ Ἀχαιοῖς ἄλγε᾽ ἔθηκε,
πολλὰς δ᾽ ἰφθίμους ψυχὰς Ἄϊδι προΐαψεν
ἡρώων, αὐτοὺς δὲ ἑλώρια τεῦχε κύνεσσιν
5οἰωνοῖσί τε πᾶσι, Διὸς δ᾽ ἐτελείετο βουλή,
ἐξ οὗ δὴ τὰ πρῶτα διαστήτην ἐρίσαντε
Ἀτρεΐδης τε ἄναξ ἀνδρῶν καὶ δῖος Ἀχιλλεύς.
τίς τ᾽ ἄρ σφωε θεῶν ἔριδι ξυνέηκε μάχεσθαι;
Λητοῦς καὶ Διὸς υἱός: ὃ γὰρ βασιλῆϊ χολωθεὶς
10νοῦσον ἀνὰ στρατὸν ὄρσε κακήν, ὀλέκοντο δὲ λαοί

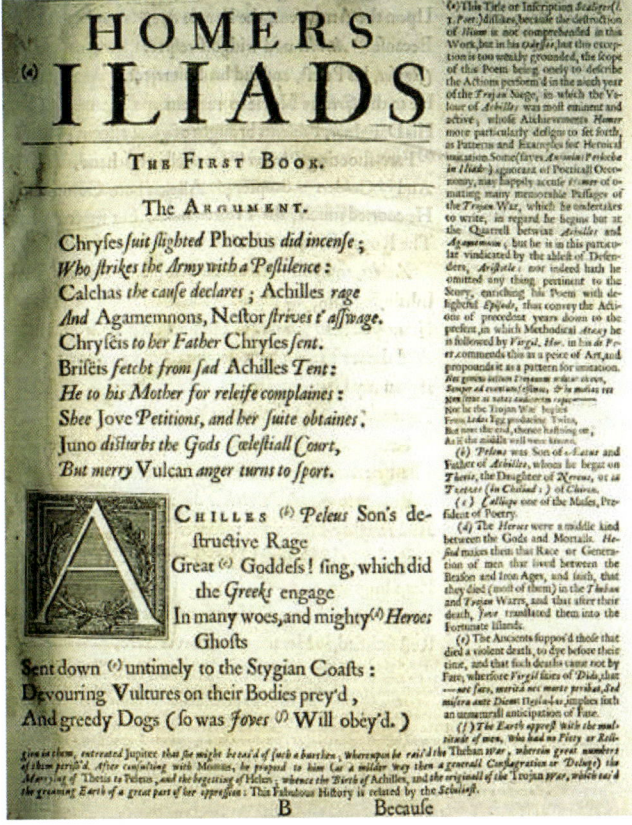

Homerus. Homer, Iliad, translated by John Ogilby. London, Printed by Thomas Roycroft, 1660.

IL.20,10. Zeus in meeting with the other gods;
Greeks and Trojans in battle

.

Achilles Peleus Son's destructive Rage.
Great Goddess, sing, which did the Greeks engage
In many Woes, and mighty Hero's Ghosts
Sent down untimely to the Stygian Coasts:
Devouring Vultures on their Bodies prey'd
And greedy Dogs (so was Jove's Will obeyed;)
Because Great Agamemnon fell at odds
With stern Achilles, Off-spring of the Gods,

Ogilby, John, London. 1669.

μῆνιν ἄειδε θεὰ Πηληϊάδεω Ἀχιλῆος
οὐλομένην, ἣ μυρί᾽ Ἀχαιοῖς ἄλγε᾽ ἔθηκε,
πολλὰς δ᾽ ἰφθίμους ψυχὰς Ἄϊδι προΐαψεν
ἡρώων, αὐτοὺς δὲ ἑλώρια τεῦχε κύνεσσιν
5οἰωνοῖσί τε πᾶσι, Διὸς δ᾽ ἐτελείετο βουλή,
ἐξ οὗ δὴ τὰ πρῶτα διαστήτην ἐρίσαντε
Ἀτρεΐδης τε ἄναξ ἀνδρῶν καὶ δῖος Ἀχιλλεύς.

Rating

οὐλομένην	-1	destructive
προΐαψεν	-1	Sent down untimely
ἑλώρια	+1	Devouring Vultures .. prey'd
Overall	-1	

HOBBES

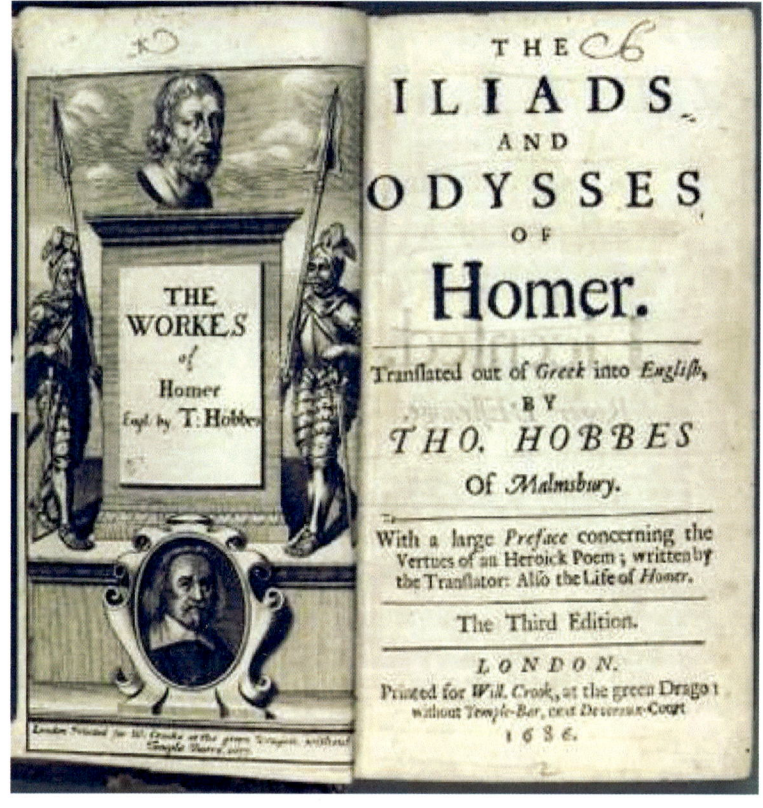

Homer, *The Iliads and Odysses of Homer* translated out of Greek into
English by Tho. Hobbes. London: Will Crook, 1686

O goddess sing what woe the discontent
Of Thetis' son brought to the Greeks; what souls
Of heroes down to Erebus it sent,
Leaving their bodies unto dogs and fowls;
Whilst the two princes of the army strove,
King Agamemnon and Achilles stout,
That so it should be was the will of Jove,
But who was he that made them first fall out?
Apollo; who incensed by the wrong
To his priest Chryses by Atrides done,
Sent a great pestilence the Greeks among;
Apace they died, and remedy was none.
Thomas Hobbes, Thucydides, Homer, J. Bohn, 1844, The English works of Thomas Hobbes of Malmesbury, Volume 10

μῆνιν ἄειδε θεὰ Πηληϊάδεω Ἀχιλῆος
οὐλομένην, ἣ μυρί' Ἀχαιοῖς ἄλγε' ἔθηκε,
πολλὰς δ' ἰφθίμους ψυχὰς Ἄϊδι προΐαψεν
ἡρώων, αὐτοὺς δὲ ἑλώρια τεῦχε κύνεσσιν
5οἰωνοῖσί τε πᾶσι, Διὸς δ' ἐτελείετο βουλή,
ἐξ οὗ δὴ τὰ πρῶτα διαστήτην ἐρίσαντε
Ἀτρεΐδης τε ἄναξ ἀνδρῶν καὶ δῖος Ἀχιλλεύς.
τίς τ' ἄρ σφωε θεῶν ἔριδι ξυνέηκε μάχεσθαι;
Λητοῦς καὶ Διὸς υἱός: ὃ γὰρ βασιλῆϊ χολωθεὶς
10νοῦσον ἀνὰ στρατὸν ὄρσε κακήν, ὀλέκοντο δὲ λαοί

Rating

οὐλομένην	-1	discontent
προΐαψεν	-1	sent
ἑλώρια	-1	Leaving their bodies unto
Overall	-3	

"Some sense of Hobbes's manner can be derived from his version of the opening of the Iliad [...] Hobbes provided understanding, unpretentious versions of Homer's narratives". The Oxford History of Literary Translation in English: 1660-1790, Stuart Gillespie, David Hopkins, Oxford University Press, 2005

Pope criticized Hobbes' translation as follows: "but for particulars and circumstance he continually lops them, and often omits the most beautiful. . . . He sometimes omits whole similes and sentences. . . ."

POPE

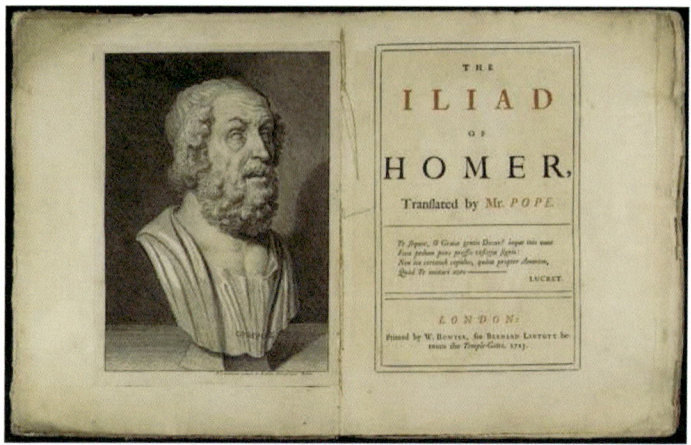

The Iliad of Homer, translated by Alexander Pope

THE Wrath of Peleus' Son, the direful Spring
Of all the Grecian Woes, O Goddess, sing!
That Wrath which hurl'd to Pluto's gloomy Reign
The Souls of mighty Chiefs untimely slain;
Whose Limbs unbury'd on the naked Shore
Devouring Dogs and hungry Vultures tore.
Since Great Achilles and Atrides strove,
Such was the Sov'reign Doom, and such the Will of Jove.
Declare, O Muse! in what ill-fated Hour
Sprung the fierce Strife, from what offended Pow'r?
Latona's Son a dire Contagion spread,
And heap'd the Camp with Mountains of the Dead;

The Iliad of Homer, translated by Alexander Pope,1763

μῆνιν ἄειδε θεὰ Πηληϊάδεω Ἀχιλῆος
οὐλομένην, ἣ μυρί' Ἀχαιοῖς ἄλγε' ἔθηκε,
πολλὰς δ' ἰφθίμους ψυχὰς Ἄϊδι προΐαψεν
ἡρώων, αὐτοὺς δὲ ἑλώρια τεῦχε κύνεσσιν
5οἰωνοῖσί τε πᾶσι, Διὸς δ' ἐτελείετο βουλή,
ἐξ οὗ δὴ τὰ πρῶτα διαστήτην ἐρίσαντε
Ἀτρεΐδης τε ἄναξ ἀνδρῶν καὶ δῖος Ἀχιλλεύς.
τίς τ' ἄρ σφωε θεῶν ἔριδι ξυνέηκε μάχεσθαι;
Λητοῦς καὶ Διὸς υἱός: ὃ γὰρ βασιλῆϊ χολωθεὶς
10νοῦσον ἀνὰ στρατὸν ὄρσε κακήν, ὀλέκοντο δὲ λαοί

Rating

οὐλομένην	+0.5	direful Spring
προΐαψεν	+1	hurl'd
ἑλώρια	+1	Devouring .. tore
Overall	+2.5	

Arnold quotes Bentley referring to Pope's translation of the Iliad as "a pretty poem, but must not be called Homer". (Arnold, M., 1960). Pope renders the criterion terms of the present book correctly.

MACPHERSON

THE wrath of the son of Peleus,—O goddess of
song, unfold! The deadly wrath of Achilles; To
Greece the source of many woes! Which peopled
the regions of death,—with shades of heroes untimely slain:
While pale they lay along the shore: Torn by beasts and
birds of prey: But such was the will of Jove! Begin the
verse, from the source of rage,—between Achilles and the
sovereign of men.
Who of the gods was HE? Who kindled rage between
the chiefs? Who, but the son of Latona and high-thunder-
ing Jove? He—rouzed to wrath against the king,—threw
death and disease, among the host. The people perished

The Iliad of Homer, Translated by James Macpherson, Esq. London, 1773

Rating

οὐλομένην	-1	deadly
προΐαψεν	-1	untimely slain
ἑλώρια	+1	Torn
Overall	-1	

"James Macpherson's *Iliad* of 1773 is unreadable but significant in
its attempt to forge (perhaps the most *Juste*) an 'epic prose', Biblical
and formulaic, in which to convey Homer's voice."
(Fowler, R. L. 2004).

Referring to Macpherson's *Iliad* the *Edinburg Magazine or Literary
Miscellany for July 1796* writes: "fraught with vanity and self-
consequence, and which met with the most mortifying reception
from the public. It was condemned by the critics, ridiculed by the
wits, and neglected by the world."

COWPER

Achilles sing, O Goddess! Peleus' son;
His wrath pernicious, who ten thousand woes
Caused to Achaia's host, sent many a soul
Illustrious into Ades premature,
And Heroes gave (so stood the will of Jove)
To dogs and to all ravening fowls a prey,
When fierce dispute had separated once
The noble Chief Achilles from the son
Of Atreus, Agamemnon, King of men.
 Who them to strife impell'd? What power divine?
Latona's son and Jove's. For he, incensed
Against the King, a foul contagion raised
In all the host, and multitudes destroy'd,
For that the son of Atreus had his priest
Dishonored, Chryses. To the fleet he came

The Iliad of Homer, Translated into English Blank Verse by William
Cowper. New York, 1860

Rating

οὐλομένην	-1	pernicious
προΐαψεν	-1	sent premature
ἑλώρια	-1	prey
Overall	-3	

NEWMAN

Of Peleus' son, Achilles, sing, oh goddess, the resentment
Accursed, which with countless pangs Achaia's army
wounded,
And forward flung to Aides full many a gallant spirit
Of heroes, and their very selves did toss to dogs that ravin,
And unto every fowl, (for so would Jove's device be
compass'd);
From that first day when feud arose implacable, and parted
The son of Atreus, prince of men, and Achileus the godlike.
Which of the gods entangled you in wrathfulness of quarrel ?
Jove and Latona's son it was, who, with the king embitter'd,
Sent mid the army sore disease, till troop on troop would
perish:

The Iliad of Homer Faithfully Translated to Unrhymed English Metre by
F.W. Newman. London, 1856

Rating

ούλομένην	-1	Accursed
προΐαψεν	+1	forward flung
έλώρια	+1	toss to dogs that ravin
Overall	+1	

EARL OF DERBY

Of Peleus' son, Achilles, sing, O Muse,
The vengeance, deep and deadly; whence to Greece
Unnumbered ills arose; which many a soul
Of mighty warriors to the viewless shades
Untimely sent; they on the battle plain
Unburied lay, a prey to rav'ning dogs,
And carrion birds; but so had Jove decreed,
From that sad day when first in wordy war,
The mighty Agamemnon, King of men,
Confronted stood by Peleus' godlike son.

Say then, what God the fatal strife provok'd?
Jove's and Latona's son; he, filled with wrath
Against the King, with deadly pestilence
The camp afflicted,--and the people died,--

The Iliad of Homer rendered into English blank verse. To which are appended translations of poems ancient and modern. Edward George Geoffrey Smith Stanley Derby, Earl of, London: Murray, 1867.

Rating

οὐλομένην	-1	deep and deadly
προΐαψεν	-1	Untimely sent
ἑλώρια	+1	prey to rav'ning
Overall	-1	

BRYANT

GODDESS! sing the wrath of Peleus' son,
Achilles; sing the deadly wrath that brought
Woes numberless upon the Greeks, and swept
To Hades many a valiant soul, and gave
Their limbs a prey to dogs and birds of air,
For so had Jove appointed, — from the time
When the two chiefs, Atrides, king of men
And great Achilles, parted first as foes.
Which of the gods put strife between the chiefs.
That they should thus contend? Latona's son
And Jove's. Incensed against the king, he bade
A deadly pestilence appear among
The army, and the men were perishing.

The Iliad of Homer, Translated into English Blank Verse, by William
Cullen Bryant, Boston, 1871

Rating

οὐλομένην	-1	deadly
προΐαψεν	+1	swept
ἐλώρια	-1	prey
Overall	-1	

MYERS

Sing, goddess, the wrath of Achilles Peleus' son, the ruinous wrath that brought on the Achaians woes innumerable, and hurled down into Hades many strong souls of heroes, and gave their bodies to be a prey to dogs and all winged fowl; and so the counsel of Zeus wrought out its accomplishment from the day when first parted Atrides king of men and noble Achiles.

Who then among the gods set the twain at strife and variance? Even the son of Leto and of Zeus; for he in anger at the king sent a sore plague upon the host, that the folk began to perish,

The Iliad of Homer Done in English Prose by Andrew Lang, M.A., Walter Leaf, M.A., and Earnest Myers, M.A., London 1883

Rating

οὐλομένην	-1	ruinous
προΐαψεν	+1	hurled down
ἑλώρια	-1	prey
Overall	-1	

BUTLER

Sing, O goddess, the anger of Achilles son of Peleus, that brought countless ills upon the Achaeans. Many a brave soul [psukhê] did it send hurrying down to Hades, and many a hero did it yield a prey to dogs

and vultures, for so was the will of Zeus fulfilled from the day on which the son of Atreus, king of men, and great Achilles, first fell out with one another. And which of the gods was it that set them on to quarrel? It was the son of Zeus and Leto; for he was angry with the king

and sent a pestilence upon the host to plague the people

Homer. The Iliad of Homer. Rendered into English prose for the use of those who cannot read the original. Samuel Butler. Longmans, Green and Co. 39 Paternoster Row, London. New York and Bombay. 1898 (?)

Rating

οὐλομένην	-2	-
προΐαψεν	+1	send hurrying down
ἐλώρια	-1	prey
Overall	-2	

MURRAY

The wrath sing, goddess, of Peleus' son, Achilles, that destructive wrath which brought countless woes upon the Achaeans, and sent forth to Hades many valiant souls of heroes, and made them themselves spoil for dogs and every bird; thus the plan of Zeus came to fulfillment, [5] from the time when1 first they parted in strife Atreus' son, king of men, and brilliant Achilles. Who then of the gods was it that brought these two together to contend? The son of Leto and Zeus; for he in anger against the king roused throughout the host an evil pestilence, and the people began to perish, [10] because upon the priest Chryses the son of Atreus had wrought dishonour.

Homer. The Iliad with an English Translation by A.T. Murray, Ph.D. in two volumes. Cambridge, MA., Harvard University Press; London, William Heinemann, Ltd. 1924.

Rating

οὐλομένην	-1	destructive
προΐαψεν	-1	sent forth
ἐλώρια	-1	spoil
Overall	-3	

ROUSE

AN ANGRY MAN - THERE IS MY STORY: THE BITTER RANCOUR
OF
Achilles, prince of the house of Peleus, which brought a
thousand troubles upon the Achaian host. Many a strong soul it
sent down to Hades, and left the heroes themselves a prey to
dogs and carrion birds, while the will of God moved on to fulfil-
ment.
It began first of all with a quarrel between my Lord King
Agamemnon of Atreus' line and the Prince Achilles.
What god, then, made the feud between them? Apollo, son
of Leto and Zeus. The King had offended him: so he sent a
dire
pestilence on the camp and the people perished.

Homer, The Iliad, The Story of Achilles. Translated by W. H. D. Rouse,
1956 (Seventh printing of the 1950 edition. First edition: 1938)

Rating

οὐλομένην	-1	BITTER
προΐαψεν	-1	sent down
ἐλώρια	-1	prey
Overall	-3	

LATTIMORE

IL.1.1   μῆνιν ἄειδε θεὰ Πηληϊάδεω Ἀχιλῆος
IL.1.1   SING, goddess, the anger of Peleus' son Achilleus
IL.1.2   οὐλομένην, ἣ μυρί' Ἀχαιοῖς ἄλγε' ἔθηκε,
IL.1.2   and its devastation, which put pains thousandfold upon the
Achaians,
IL.1.3   πολλὰς δ' ἰφθίμους ψυχὰς Ἄϊδι προΐαψεν
IL.1.3   hurled in their multitudes to the house of Hades strong souls
IL.1.4   ἡρώων, αὐτοὺς δὲ ἑλώρια τεῦχε κύνεσσιν
IL.1.4   of heroes, but gave their bodies to be the delicate feasting
IL.1.5   οἰωνοῖσί τε πᾶσι, Διὸς δ' ἐτελείετο βουλή,
IL.1.5   of dogs, of all birds, and the will of Zeus was accomplished
IL.1.6   ἐξ οὗ δὴ τὰ πρῶτα διαστήτην ἐρίσαντε
IL.1.6   since that time when first there stood in division of conflict
IL.1.7   Ἀτρεΐδης τε ἄναξ ἀνδρῶν καὶ δῖος Ἀχιλλεύς.
IL.1.7   Atreus' son the lord of men and brilliant Achilleus.
IL.1.8   τίς τ' ἄρ σφωε θεῶν ἔριδι ξυνέηκε μάχεσθαι;
IL.1.8   What god was it then set them together in bitter collision?
IL.1.9   Λητοῦς καὶ Διὸς υἱός: ὃ γὰρ βασιλῆϊ χολωθεὶς
IL.1.9   Zeus' son and Leto's, Apollo, who in anger at the king drove
IL.1.10   νοῦσον ἀνὰ στρατὸν ὦρσε κακήν, ὀλέκοντο δὲ λαοί,
IL.1.10   the foul pestilence along the host, and the people perished

Iliad. Richmond Lattimore, 1951. Digital edition
http://digital.library.northwestern.edu/homer/html/application.html

Rating

οὐλομένην	+1	devastation
προΐαψεν	+1	hurled
ἑλώρια	-1	delicate feasting
Overall	+1	

REES

Sing, O Goddess, the ruinous wrath of Achilles,
Son of Peleus, the terrible curse that brought
Unnumbered woes upon the Achaeans and hurled
To Hades so many heroic souls, leaving
Their bodies the prey of dogs and carrion birds.
The will of Zeus was done from the moment they quarreled,
Agamemnon, son of Atreus, and godlike Achilles.
　　Which of the gods caused two such men to contend?
The son of Zeus and Leto. Deeply incensed
With King Agamemnon for failing to honor Chryses
His priest, Apollo sent a plague on the soldiers,
And many people were dying

The Iliad of Homer, Translated by Ennis Rees (first printing 1963)

Rating

οὐλομένην	-1	ruinous
προΐαψεν	+1	hurled
ἑλώρια	-1	prey
Overall	-1	

FITZGERALD

ANGER be now your song, immortal one,
Achilles' anger, doomed and ruinous,
that caused the Achaeans loss on bitter loss
and crowded brave souls into the undergloom,
leaving so many dead men-carrion
for dogs and birds and the will of Zeus was done.
Begin it when the two men first contending
broke with one another-the Lord Marshal
Agamemnon, Atreus' son and Prince Achilles.
  Among the gods, who brought this quarrel on?
The son of Zeus by Leto. Agamemnon
angered him, so he made a burning wind
of plague rise in the army; rank and file
sickened and died

Homer, The Iliad. Translation C. Robert Fitzgerald, Oxford University
Press, 1998 (Revised edition of the first edition of 1974).

Rating

οὐλομένην	+1	doomed and ruinous
προΐαψεν	-1	crowded
ἑλώρια	-1	carrion
Overall	-1	

FAGLES

Rage - Goddess, sing the rage of Peleus' son Achilles,
murderous, doomed, that cost the Achaeans countless losses,
hurling down to the house of Death so many sturdy souls,
great fighters' souls, but made their bodies carrion,
feasts for dogs and birds,
and the will of Zeus was moving toward its end.
Begin, Muse, when the two first broke and clashed,
Agamemnon lord of men and brilliant Achilles.
     What god drove them to fight with such a fury?
Apollo the son of Zeus and Leto. Incensed at the king
he swept a fatal plague through the army - men were dying

Homer, The Iliad. Robert Fagles, 1991 (second edition of the New York,
1990 first edition).

Rating

οὐλομένην	+1	murderous, doomed
προΐαψεν	+1	hurling down
ἑλώρια	-1	carrion
Overall	+1	

RECK

Sing, Goddess, Achilles' maniac rage:
ruinous thing! it roused a thousand sorrows
and hurled many souls of mighty warriors
to Hades, made their bodies food to dogs
and carrion birds - as Zeus's will foredoomed-
from the time relentless strife came between
Atreus's son, king, and brave Achilles.
  Which immortal brought about that quarrel?
None but Apollo-he sent pestilence
to ravage the Achaeans: indignant
Agamemnon has spurned the priest Chryses

The Iliad. Michael Pierce Reck, 1994

Rating

οὐλομένην	-1	ruinous
προΐαψεν	+1	hurled
ἑλώρια	-1	carrion
Overall	-1	

LOMBARDO

RAGE:
  Sing, Goddess, Achilles' rage,
Black and murderous, that cost the Greeks
Incalculable pain, pitched countless souls
of heroes into Hades' dark,
And left their bodies to rot as feast
For dogs and birds, as Zeus' will was done.
  Begin with the clash between Agamemnon-
The Greek warlord-and godlike Achilles.

  Which of the immortals set these two
At each other's throats?
                Apollo,
Zeus' son and Leto's, offended
By the warlord. Agamemnon had dishonored
Chryses, Apollo's priest, so the god
Struck the Greek camp with plague,
And the soldiers were dying of it.

Iliad, Homer, Translated by Stanley Lombardo
Hackett Publishing, 1997

Rating

οὐλομένην	-1	Black and murderous
προΐαψεν	+1	pitched
ἐλώρια	-1	feast
Overall	-1	

COMPARATIVE CRITICISM

CRITICISM LINE BY LINE

The Latin text comes from *Ilias, graece et latine.*
Ex recensione et cum notis Samuelis Clarke.
Nova ed. Published 1845 by R. Martin in Edinburgi.
Written in Latin.

LINE ONE

μῆνιν ἄειδε θεὰ Πηληϊάδεω Ἀχιλῆος
Iram cane, Dea Pelidae Achillis

I Thee beseech, O Goddesse milde, the hatefull hate to plaine
(Hall, 1581)
ACHILLES' baneful wrath resound, O Goddess, that impos'd
(Chapman, 1612)
O goddess sing what woe the discontent Of Thetis' son
(Hobbes, 1686)
Achilles Peleus Son's destructive Rage. Great Goddess, sing
(Ogilby, 1669)
THE Wrath of Peleus' Son, the direful Spring
Of all the Grecian Woes, O Goddess, sing! (Pope 1763?)
THE wrath of the son of Peleus,—O goddess of
song, unfold! The deadly wrath of Achilles (Macpherson,
1773)
Achilles sing, O Goddess! Peleus' son; His wrath (Cowper,
1791)
Of Peleus' son, Achilles, sing, oh goddess, the resentment
(Newman, 1856)
Of Peleus' son, Achilles, sing, O Muse, The vengeance (Earl
of Derby, 1867)
GODDESS! sing the wrath of Peleus' son, Achilles (Bryant,
1870)
Sing, goddess, the wrath of Achilles Peleus' son (Myers, 1883)
Sing, O goddess, the anger of Achilles son of Peleus (Butler,
1898)

The wrath do thou sing, O goddess, of Peleus' son, Achilles (Murray, 1924)

AN ANGRY MAN - THERE IS MY STORY: THE BITTER RANCOUR OF Achilles (Rouse, 1938)

SING, goddess, the anger of Peleus' son Achilleus (Lattimore, 1951)

Sing, O Goddess, the ruinous wrath of Achilles, Son of Peleus (Rees, 1963)

ANGER be now your song, immortal one, Achilles' anger (Fitzgerald. 1974)

Rage - Goddess, sing the rage of Peleus' son Achilles (Fagles, 1990)

Sing, Goddess, Achilles' maniac rage (Reck, 1994)

RAGE: Sing, Goddess, Achilles' rage (Lombardo, 1997)

In the opening line of the Iliad, the listener's attention is drawn on one word "μῆνιν", which belongs to Achilleus. Homer's intention is to trigger the image of Achilleus in a certain emotional state, a state that presumably fuels the events that follow. The success or failure of any translation of this line depends upon this fact. The translator's task is to focus on this word, and render the meaning of the word correctly.

Pope translates "μῆνιν" as "discontent", a choice that is most irrelevant. Hall translates "μῆνιν" as "hate", which misses the character of the emotion in question. I can hate someone without being enraged. Similarly, Newman's translation as "discontent" misses the correct meaning of rage. The same argument applies to "of vengeance ", the translation of the Earl of Derby.

"Anger" is a poor choice (Butler, Rouse, Lattimore, Fitzgerald), "wrath" (Chapman, Pope, Macpherson, Cowper, Bryant, Myers, Murray, Rees) is a better choice, "rage" is even better (Ogilby, Fagles, Lombardo) but still not accurate.; "maniac rage" is the best rendition (Reck).

"μῆνις" is not simple anger, or wrath, it relates to "μένος?", a rage that possess one for a long time (ἐπιμένουσα ὀργή, ἐκ τοῦ μένειν, οὑμὴν ἐκ τοῦ μαίνεσθαι). The only translator that succeeds with this issue is Reck.

Hall's "I Thee beseech, O Goddesse" is a translation of the French text "JE TE Supply Deeffe ".

Ranking
1 (Best) Reck
2. Fagles
3. Ogilby, Lombardo
4. Chapman, Pope, Macpherson, Cowper, Bryant, Myers, Murray, Rees

5. Butler, Rouse, Lattimore, Fitzgerald
6. Newman, Earl of Derby
7. Hobbes, Pope
8. (Worst) Hall, Rouse

LINE TWO

οὐλομένην, ἣ μυρί᾽ Ἀχαιοῖς ἄλγε᾽ ἔθηκε
Perniciosam, quae infinitos Achivis dolores fecit
the hateful hate to plaine,
Whereby Achilles was so wroong, and grewe in suche
disdaine, (Hall, 1581)
that impos'd Infinite sorrows on the Greeks (Chapman, 1612)
what woe the discontent Of Thetis' son brought to the Greeks
(Hobbes, 1686)
destructive Rage.
Great Goddess, sing, which did the Greeks engage In many
Woes (Ogilby, 1669)
THE Wrath of Peleus' Son, the direful Spring
Of all the Grecian Woes, O Goddess, sing! (Pope 1763?)
The deadly wrath of Achilles; To Greece the source of many
woes (Macpherson, 1773)
His wrath pernicious, who ten thousand woes Caused to
Achaia's host (Cowper, 1791)
the resentment Accursed, which with countless pangs Achaia's
army wounded (Newman, 1856)
The vengeance, deep and deadly; whence to Greece
Unnumbered ills arose (Earl of Derby, 1867)
sing the deadly wrath that brought Woes numberless upon the
Greeks (Bryant, 1870)
the ruinous wrath that brought on the Achaians woes
innumerable (Myers, 1883)
that brought countless ills upon the Achaeans (Butler, 1898)
that baneful wrath which brought countless woes upon the
Achaeans (Murray, 1924)
THE BITTER RANCOUR [...], which brought a thousand
troubles upon the Achaian host (Rouse, 1938)
and its devastation, which put pains thousandfold upon the
Achaians (Lattimore, 1951)
the terrible curse that brought unnumbered woes upon the
Achaeans (Rees, 1963)
94

doomed and ruinous, that caused the Achaeans loss on bitter
loss (Fitzgerald, 1974)
murderous, doomed, that cost the Achaeans countless losses
(Fagles, 1990)
ruinous thing! it roused a thousand sorrows (Reck, 1994)
Black and murderous, that cost the Greeks Incalculable pain
(Lombardo, 1997)

The function of the second line is twofold: one, to draw
attention once again to "μηνιν", manic rage, and characterize it
as "ουλομένην", baneful? and, two, to inform that this rage put
pains on the Achaeans.

Translating the word "ουλομένην" is not an easy matter. At the
core of the word is the meaning of "perishing" or "loss" as in
death. The meaning proposed by the present author, that of
loss, is supported by the same image of loss, perishing, in
ὀλέκοντο δὲ λαοί, Hom. Il. 1.10

οὐλομένην, poetic form of ὀλομένην (verb ὄλλυμι, to lose,
destroy, be lost, perish to destroy, make an end of). Οὐλόμενος
is wrongly translated as "accursed" in Perseus.

Poetical ὀλέκω; of things, to be lost
ἄνερ ἀπ᾽ αἰῶνος νέος ὤλεο, Hom. Il. 24.725
τὴν ἄρετ᾽ ἐξ ἐνάρων πόλιν Ἡετίωνος ὀλέσσας: Hom. Il. 9.188

εἰ μέν κ᾽ αὖθι μένων Τρώων πόλιν ἀμφιμάχωμαι,
ὤλετο μέν μοι νόστος, ἀτὰρ κλέος ἄφθιτον ἔσται:
εἰ δέ κεν οἴκαδ᾽ ἵκωμι φίλην ἐς πατρίδα γαῖαν,
ὤλετό μοι κλέος ἐσθλόν, ἐπὶ δηρὸν δέ μοι αἰὼν
ἔσσεται, οὐδέ κέ μ᾽ ὦκα τέλος θανάτοιο κιχείη. Hom. Il.
9.412-416

μη και χρόα καλόν ολέσσω (Theocritus Idyl. xxvii, 30)

95

The Latin translation (*Ilias Latina*) renders "ουλομένην" as *perniciosa*. It is surprising that of those translators we include here, only Cowper uses the term "pernicious".
"*Pernicies* has an active meaning and denotes the destruction of a living being by murder; whereas *exitium* has a passive meaning, and denotes the destruction even of lifeless objects by annihilation"
"Poppea non nise in perniciem uxoris nupta (Tacito, Annali, xiv, 6,5)

per-nicies; from nex, necis=violent death
necare=kill
internecio=massacre
perniciosus; deadly, dangerous

A synonym of *perniciosa* is "fatalis"; however, this may convey the meaning of fate, which should be avoided. The translation I propose here should convey the image of been lost, one that has perished as in death, annihilated. Interestingly in Modern Greek, this can be rendered, as for example it has been done by poet Nikos Kavvadias: "ταξείδι του χαμού".

In reference to the rage, the image that Homer wants to pass across is this: rage is seen as an agent, which put, "έθηκε", myriads of pains on the Achaeans. I believe that the primary goal of a translator is to try to pass the original images as much as possible, as this touches the very core of poetry. Good poetry communicates with images, juxtaposed, without explicit causal connections, as, for example, in Camus. Homer's poetry has set the stage for this principle. Sacrificing this principle for the sake of rhyming or acrobatics in language leads to poor translation.

Ranking

Reference to "ουλομένην"

Some translators omit this word (Chapman, Hobbes, Butler). Most translators use epithets that convey the negative, destructive quality of the rage:
hateful (Hall), destructive (Ogilby), direful (Pope), deadly (Macpherson), pernicious (Cowper), accursed (Newman), deep and deadly (Earl of Derby), deadly (Bryant), ruinous (Myers), baneful (Murray), bitter (Rouse), devastation (Lattimore), terrible curse (Rees), doomed and ruinous (Fitzgerald), murderous, doomed (Fagles), Black and murderous (Lombardo)

None of the translations is successful.

1. (Best) Lattimore
2. (Bad) All the rest
3. (Worst) Hall

Reference to "ἔθηκε"

grew (Hall), imposed (Chapman), brought (Hobbes, Bryant, Myers, Butler, Murray, Rouse, Rees), put upon (Lattimore), engage (Ogilby), source, spring (Pope, Macpherson), rose (Earl of Derby, Reck), cost (Fagles, Lombardo), caused (Cowper, Fitzgerald), wounded (Newman)

1. (Best) Lattimore
2. Hobbes, Bryant, Myers, Butler, Murray, Rouse, Rees
3. Chapman
4. Pope, Macpherson
5. Earl of Derby, Reck
6. Ogilby, Fagles, Lombardo

7. Cowper, Fitzgerald
8. Hall, Newman

Reference to "ἄλγεα"

sorrows (Chapman, Reck), woe (Hobbes, Ogilby, Pope, Macpherson, Cowper, Bryant, Myers, Murray, Rees), pangs (Newman), ills (Earl of Derby, Butler), troubles (Rouse), pains (Lattimore, Lombardo), loss (Fitzgerald, Fagles)

"'ἄλγος" is pain, physical pain, and secondarily psychological pain.

1. (Best) Lattimore, Lombardo
2. Chapman, Reck, Hobbes, Ogilby, Pope, Macpherson, Cowper, Bryant, Myers, Murray, Rees, Newman, Earl of Derby, Butler, Rouse
3. Fitzgerald, Fagles

LINE THREE

πολλὰς δ᾽ ἰφθίμους ψυχὰς Ἄϊδι προΐαψεν
Multasque fortes animas orco praemature misit
That thousandes of the Greekish Dukes, in hard and heauie plight,
To Plutoes Courte did yeelde their soules (Hall, 1581)
and many bravo souls los'd From breasts heroic; sent them far
to that invisible cave That no light comforts (Chapman, 1612)
what souls Of heroes down to Erebus it sent (Hobbes, 1686)
and mighty Hero's Ghosts
Sent down untimely to the Stygian Coasts (Ogilby, 1669)
That Wrath which hurl'd to Pluto's gloomy Reign
The Souls of mighty Chiefs untimely slain (Pope 1763?)
Which peopled
the regions of death,—with shades of heroes untimely slain (Macpherson, 1773)
sent many a soul Illustrious into Ades premature (Cowper, 1791)
And forward flung to Aides full many a gallant spirit
Of heroes (Newman, 1856)
which many a soul Of mighty warriors to the viewless shades
Untimely sent (Earl of Derby, 1867)
and swept To Hades many a valiant soul (Bryant, 1870)
and
hurled down into Hades many strong souls of heroes (Myers, 1883)
Many a brave soul [psukhê] did it send hurrying down to Hades (Butler, 1898)
and sent forth to Hades
many valiant souls of warriors (Murray, 1924)
Many a strong soul it sent down to Hades (Rouse, 1938)
 hurled in their multitudes to the house of Hades strong souls (Lattimore, 1951)
and hurled To Hades so many heroic souls (Rees, 1963)
and crowded brave souls into the undergloom (Fitzgerald.
99

1974)
hurling down to the house of Death so many sturdy souls
(Fagles, 1990)
and hurled many souls of mighty warriors
to Hades (Reck, 1994)
pitched countless souls
of heroes into Hades' dark (Lombardo, 1997)

The third line is about one picture: souls of heroes on their way to the underworld. However, it is not clear in what way they head for Hades; are they sent, hurled, sent prematurely, pitched? The verb in question is προΐαψεν.

προΐαψεν, verb προιάπτω, to send forward. Some authors take this to mean prematurely, untimely. However, προ- can be there merely for emphasis.

Eustathius poses the argument that προΐαψεν does not indicate simply sending or sending forth but it indicates damage "φθοράν καί βλάβην" because it comes from ίπτω.
cf. Πολυδίπσιον. Πολυίψιον=πολυβλαβές

ίπτω=βλάπτω
εν νόσω ετέκτυτο ου χρόα καλόν ίαψεν
ευμμελίης του δ' ου χρόα καλόν ίαψεν
Concordantia in Quinti Smyrnaei Posthomerica, Volume 2, Manolēs Papathōmopoulos, Quintus (Smyrnaeus), Olms-Weidmann, 2002

The translations we are sampling in this book render it as follows:

yeelde (Hall), sent far (Chapman), sent down (Hobbes, Rouse), sent down untimely (Ogilby) hurled untimely (Pope), peopled untimely (Macpherson), sent prematurely (Cowper), forward flung (Newman), untimely sent (Earl of Derby), swept (Bryant), hurled down (Myers, Fagles,), sent hurrying down (Butler), sent forth (Murray), hurled (Lattimore, Reese, Reck), crowded (Fitzgerald), pitched (Lombardo)
I consider the terms "hurled", "flung", "pitched" successful translations.

LINE FOUR

ἡρώων, αὐτοὺς δὲ ἑλώρια τεῦχε κύνεσσιν
Heroum, ipsosque praedam-discerpendam fecit canibus
Those sencelesse trunckes of buriall voide, by them erst gaily borne,
By rauening curres, and carreine foules, in peeces to be torne (Hall, 1581)
and their limbs to dogs and vultures gave (Chapman, 1612)
Leaving their bodies unto dogs and fowls (Hobbes, 1686)
Devouring Vultures on their Bodies prey'd And greedy Dogs (Ogilby, 1669)
Whose Limbs unbury'd on the naked Shore
Devouring Dogs and hungry Vultures tore (Pope 1763?)
While pale they lay along the shore: Torn by beasts and birds of prey (Macpherson, 1773)
And Heroes gave […] To dogs and to all ravening fowls a prey (Cowper, 1791)
Of heroes, and their very selves did toss to dogs that ravin (Newman, 1856)
they on the battle plain Unburied lay, a prey to rav'ning dogs (Earl of Derby, 1867)
and gave Their limbs a prey to dogs (Bryant, 1870)
of heroes, and gave their bodies to be a prey to dogs (Myers, 1883)
and many a hero did it yield a prey to dogs (Butler, 1898)
and made themselves to be a spoil for dogs (Murray, 1924)
and left the heroes themselves a prey to dogs (Rouse, 1938)
of heroes, but gave their bodies to be the delicate feasting [...] of dogs (Lattimore, 1951)
leaving Their bodies the prey of dogs (Rees, 1963)
leaving so many dead men-carrion for dogs (Fitzgerald. 1974)
great fighters' souls, but made their bodies carrion, feasts for dogs (Fagles, 1990)
made their bodies food to dogs (Reck, 1994)
And left their bodies to rot as feast For dogs (Lombardo,

1997)

Line four of the Iliad paints a picture with three words: heroes, macerated bodies, dogs, ἡρώων, ἑλώρια, κύνεσσιν. This is unconditionally dramatic and horrid, and omission or alteration of these three components of the picture would detract from not only the drama, but also the spirit of Homer, as this picture is like a theme that is repeated. The impact of dead bodies lying in the battlefields on the mind of Homer is important as it adds to our attempt to build the character of the Iliad. Most of the translations fail in this line not only because their esthetic criteria are at odds with my thesis of what poetry is, but also simply because of ignorance of the Greek language. ἑλώρια is not just food or prey; it is macerated, torn bodies.

The subject-object relation is not "εδωκεν, gave" (a neutral term), but "τεῦχε" a verb that conveys meanings of "run into", "just happened to find". The bodies of the heroes are painted as torn and dismembered (ἑλώρια, a synonym of σπαράγματα, παίγνια; αὐτοὺς δὲ ἑλώρια τεῦχε).

With only three words, Homer paints a rich picture, a picture of horror, surrender to the brutality of chance events of nature. He colors it with a sprinkle of sarcasm: these torn bodies are not just prey, they are playthings of dogs. Sterilizing this scene into just "bodies made food or prey to dogs" is turning poetry into poor prose, and, summarizing, not translating Homer.

The translation proposed here finds support in the fact that Homer, elsewhere in his work, views dead bodies in this light. This is the image that Homer paints elsewhere, e.g. ἔλωρ καὶ κύρμα (Od.3.271, Il.5.488, Od.5.473).

"κάλλιπεν οἰωνοῖσιν ἔλωρ καὶ κύρμα γενέσθαι, Od.3.271
"ἀνδράσι δυσμενέεσσιν ἔλωρ καὶ κύρμα γένησθε" Il.5.488

"Πριαμίδη, μὴ δή με ἕλωρ Δαναοῖσιν ἐάσῃς κεῖσθαι" Hom. Il. 5.684

κύρμα=what I hit by chance, prey

This is how ἐλώρια is rendered in the translations we are considering here:

Latin translation (praedam-discerpendam)

trunckes to be torne (Hall), omits the term (Chapman, Hobbes), prey (Ogilby, Cowper, Bryant, Myers, Butler, Rouse, Rees) tear (Pope, Macpherson, raving (Cowper, Newman, Earl of Derby), spoil (Murray), delicate feasting (Lattimore), carrion (Fitzgerald), carrion feasts (Fagles, Lombardo), food (Reck)

Ranking

1. (best) tear (Latin translation, Hall, Pope)
2. raving (Cowper, Newman, Earl of Derby)
3. prey (Ogilby, Cowper, Bryant, Myers, Butler, Rouse, Rees)
4. spoil (Murray)
5. carrion (Fitzgerald)
6. carrion feasts (Fagles, Lombardo)
7. food (Reck)
8. term omitted (Chapman, Hobbes)

In summary, these translators render the term ἐλώρια correctly:
Arthur Hall: in peeces to be torne
de Sponde's edition: laniamenta=torn to pieces
Ogilby: Devouring Vultures .. prey'd
Pope: Devouring .. tore
Macpherson: Torn
Newman: toss to dogs that ravin
Earl of Derby: prey to rav'ning

EPILOGUE

In our search for grounds upon which to base criteria for evaluating translations of the Iliad, we gain insights in tracing the evolution of Homeric epos out of poems of heroic deeds of men, κλέα ἀνδρῶν.

It is widely accepted that the subject of the Iliad is the wrath of Achilles and its consequences. While this thesis may be justified in a philological analysis, it does not receive support in an anthropological, psychoanalytic context. The criteria in resolving this issue may not be found only in analyzing the plot of the Iliad, but rather in tracing the roots of Homeric epos, and in comparative analyses within this epos.

What is Homer trying to say? What is the motivating force, the artistic pleasure that he derives from creating these poems and conveying them to his audience? Insights regarding these questions may be found within the Iliad itself. Perhaps the *raison d'être* of the Iliad is to be found in the Iliad in scenes like this:

τῇ ὅ γε θυμὸν ἔτερπεν, ἄειδε δ᾽ ἄρα κλέα ἀνδρῶν.
Πάτροκλος δέ οἱ οἶος ἐναντίος ἧστο σιωπῇ,
δέγμενος Αἰακίδην ὁπότε λήξειεν ἀείδων,
Il. 9, 189-191

Therewith was he delighting his soul, and he sang of the glorious deeds of warriors; and Patroclus alone sat over against him in silence, waiting until Aeacus' son should cease from singing. Il. 9, 189-191 (Translation by A.T. Murray)

In the Iliad, Homer is delighting his soul as he sings of the glorious deeds of warriors. We are cast in the role of Patroclus listening to "klea andron".

In the sober, objective account of crude violence, the Iliad is not dry of lyricism. Homer succeeds in triggering aesthetic reactions in us as he describes aspects of a ruthless war machine.

In the following excerpts from Book 2 of the Iliad Homer paints pictures of the Greek army rushing to their ships intending to return home.

ὣς φάτο, τοῖσι δὲ θυμὸν ἐνὶ στήθεσσιν ὄρινε
πᾶσι μετὰ πληθὺν ὅσοι οὐ βουλῆς ἐπάκουσαν:
κινήθη δ᾽ ἀγορὴ φὴ κύματα μακρὰ θαλάσσης
145πόντου Ἰκαρίοιο, τὰ μέν τ᾽ Εὖρός τε Νότος τε
ὤρορ᾽ ἐπαΐξας πατρὸς Διὸς ἐκ νεφελάων.
ὡς δ᾽ ὅτε κινήσῃ Ζέφυρος βαθὺ λήϊον ἐλθὼν
λάβρος ἐπαιγίζων, ἐπί τ᾽ ἠμύει ἀσταχύεσσιν,
ὣς τῶν πᾶσ᾽ ἀγορὴ κινήθη: τοὶ δ᾽ ἀλαλητῷ
150νῆας ἔπ᾽ ἐσσεύοντο, ποδῶν δ᾽ ὑπένερθε κονίη
ἵστατ᾽ ἀειρομένη:
IL. 2.142-151

So spake he, and roused the hearts in the breasts of all
throughout the multitude, as many as had not heard the
council. And the gathering was stirred
like the long sea-waves of the Icarian main,
which the East Wind or the South Wind has raised,
rushing upon them from the clouds of father Zeus. And
even as when the West Wind at its coming stirreth a deep
cornfield with its violent blast, and the ears bow
thereunder, even so was all their gathering stirred, and
they with loud shouting rushed towards the ships; and
from beneath their feet the dust arose on high.
IL. 2.142-151 (Translation by A.T. Murray)

In the following excerpt, Homer paints stunningly beautiful images of the Greek army as they maneuver to attack, possessed by the spirit of war, a desire to not just kill but to butcher (διαρραῖσαι μεμαῶτες), which, he says, is sweeter than returning home.

σὺν τῇ παιφάσσουσα διέσσυτο λαὸν Ἀχαιῶν
ὀτρύνουσ᾽ ἰέναι: ἐν δὲ σθένος ὦρσεν ἑκάστῳ
καρδίῃ ἄλληκτον πολεμίζειν ἠδὲ μάχεσθαι.
τοῖσι δ᾽ ἄφαρ πόλεμος γλυκίων γένετ᾽ ἠὲ νέεσθαι
ἐν νηυσὶ γλαφυρῇσι φίλην ἐς πατρίδα γαῖαν.

ἠΰτε πῦρ ἀΐδηλον ἐπιφλέγει ἄσπετον ὕλην
οὔρεος ἐν κορυφῇς, ἕκαθεν δέ τε φαίνεται αὐγή,
ὣς τῶν ἐρχομένων ἀπὸ χαλκοῦ θεσπεσίοιο
αἴγλη παμφανόωσα δι᾽ αἰθέρος οὐρανὸν ἷκε
τῶν δ᾽ ὥς τ᾽ ὀρνίθων πετεηνῶν ἔθνεα πολλὰ
460χηνῶν ἢ γεράνων ἢ κύκνων δουλιχοδείρων
Ἀσίῳ ἐν λειμῶνι Καϋστρίου ἀμφὶ ῥέεθρα
ἔνθα καὶ ἔνθα ποτῶνται ἀγαλλόμενα πτερύγεσσι
κλαγγηδὸν προκαθιζόντων, σμαραγεῖ δέ τε λειμών,
ὣς τῶν ἔθνεα πολλὰ νεῶν ἄπο καὶ κλισιάων
ἐς πεδίον προχέοντο Σκαμάνδριον: αὐτὰρ ὑπὸ χθὼν
σμερδαλέον κονάβιζε ποδῶν αὐτῶν τε καὶ ἵππων.
ἔσταν δ᾽ ἐν λειμῶνι Σκαμανδρίῳ ἀνθεμόεντι
μυρίοι, ὅσσά τε φύλλα καὶ ἄνθεα γίγνεται ὥρῃ.

ἠΰτε μυιάων ἀδινάων ἔθνεα πολλὰ
αἵ τε κατὰ σταθμὸν ποιμνήϊον ἠλάσκουσιν
ὥρῃ ἐν εἰαρινῇ ὅτε τε γλάγος ἄγγεα δεύει,
τόσσοι ἐπὶ Τρώεσσι κάρη κομόωντες Ἀχαιοὶ
ἐν πεδίῳ ἵσταντο διαρραῖσαι μεμαῶτες.
IL. 2, 455-473

Therewith she sped dazzling throughout the host of the Achaeans, urging them to go forth; and in the heart of each man she roused strength to war and to battle without ceasing. And to them forthwith war became sweeter than to return in their hollow ships to their dear native land. Even as a consuming fire maketh a boundless forest to blaze on the peaks of a mountain, and from afar is the glare thereof to be seen, even so from their innumerable bronze, as they marched forth, went the dazzling gleam up through the sky unto the heavens.

And as the many tribes of winged fowl, wild geese or cranes or long-necked swans on the Asian mead by the streams of Caystrius, fly this way and that, glorying in their strength of wing, and with loud cries settle ever onwards, and the mead resoundeth; even so their many tribes poured forth from ships and huts into the plain of Scamander, and the earth echoed wondrously beneath the tread of men and horses. So they took their stand in the flowery mead of Scamander, numberless, as are the leaves and the flowers in their season. Even as the many tribes of swarming flies that buzz to and fro throughout the herdsman's farmstead in the season of spring, when the milk drenches the pails, even in such numbers stood the long-haired Achaeans upon the plain in the face of the men of Troy, eager to rend them asunder.
IL.2.450-473 (Translation by A.T. Murray)

The Iliad is about κλέα ἀνδρῶν, the glorious and terrible deeds of men in relation to other men, the raw content of the soul of man, but not of woman. It is a vast lagoon of dream fragments of the male unconscious haunted with eternal shadows that compete, strut, fight, kill and rape, and above all seek the approval of other men. Women are there as objects. Helen is an invention in the mind of the poet, an excuse for the brilliant acting out of the eternal contest among men.

The abduction of Helen is a plot devised by the Gods, Nature, by agents outside the control of the conscious, logical self; male is doomed to fight male. Helen never goes to Troy (Herodotus, Book II, 113-116, Euterpe, 113-116. Euripides, Ἑλένη). Even on the manifest level of the Iliad, Helen is a shadow; her character is never fully painted; Helen's *raison d'être* is the justification for the fighting of the Trojan War. The most famous war takes place for a shadow! In fact, it is an acting-out of the clashes and rituals of the archetypal shadows haunting the male soul.

Herodotus writes that Homer knew the story of Helen, that she was taken to Egypt by the gods, but he changed it in order to establish a *bona fide* cause for the war. "The priests [in Egypt] gave this account of the arrival of Helen at the court of Proteus. And Homer appears to me to have heard this relation; but it was not equally suited to epic poetry" (Herodotus, *The Histories, Book II, Euterpe,* 113-116).

Looking past the historical, theological, and literary merits of the Iliad, we find a rich psychoanalytic terrain of male identity.

A successful translation of Homer would be that which recreates the images and responses, emotional and intellectual, that Homer attempts to pass on to his audience. To agree with Arnold in part, this may not be possible. However, Arnold's statement should be qualified. Certain images and sounds, as already stated earlier, e.g. images from nature and body parts, especially those relating to reproduction, sounds and body movements, carry a phyletic impact that is not confined to a given geographical point or epoch. This is perhaps one the arguments why translators should stay close to the original and spend their energy on conveying these images and sounds as effectively as possible, rather than toiling on devising presumably poetical embellishments, thus missing or altering the *significant image*. Arnold's use of nature in his poetry shows that he is aware (at least at the unconscious level) of the power of images from nature because of their permanence and capacity to trigger the same responses in us across millennia.

In this book, I have traced the history of the Iliad from papyrus, to parchment, to paper, to e-book. Next, I have looked into the first ten lines of Book 1 in the original Homeric text, the Latin text, and lastly the English translations. A brief account of the Iliad in French and Greek (vernacular) is also given. I have chosen twenty English translations, beginning with the first translations of Hall, and Chapman. The criterion for the selection was, for the most part, dictated by what I considered important. I have evaluated these translations using criteria based on considerations discussed in this book.

Specifically, I have identified three loci at which Homer paints subtle but dramatic images in the characteristic manner of his art. These loci are:

Line 2: οὐλομένην (Il. 1.2)
Line 3: ἑλώρια (Il. 1.3)
Line 4: προΐαψεν (Il. 1.4)

Most of the translations examined in this book miss or distort the images intended by Homer.

I conclude with the statement I made in the introduction of this book. Homer has not successfully been translated into English yet; he will never be; he can only be paraphrased, and thus inspire poets to create their own worlds. All the efforts by gifted poets and scholars so far, have certainly contributed to our understanding of Homer; they have also contributed to the enrichment of English literature, but have not allowed anyone reading an English translation to experience Homer as Greek speakers can.

Prerequisites for a successful translation of the Iliad include a clear and deep understanding of its essence, and recognition that the precise rendition of *significant images*, those of phyletic meaning, has priority over poetic embellishment.

BIBLIOGRAPHY

Amos, F. R. *Early Theories of Translation*, Columbia University Press, 1920

Aristotle. ed. R. Kassel, *Aristotle's Ars Poetica*. Oxford, Clarendon Press. 1966.

Arnold, M. "On Translating Homer." In On the Classical Tradition, ed. R. H. Super. Michigan University Press, Ann Arbor and London, 1960

Bekker, I., Reimer, G., *Apollonii Sophistae Lexicon Homericum. Apollonius le Sophiste*, 1833

Bryant, W. C. *The Iliad of Homer:* translated into English blank verse, Boston, 1870.

Chalcocondyles (Δημήτριος Χαλκοκονδύλης). *Ὁμήρου τὰ σωζόμενα*, Florence 1488

Cramer, J. A. *Anecdota Graeca e codd. manuscriptis Bibliothecarum Oxoniensium.* Typographeo academico, 1835

Cureton, W. *Fragments of the Iliad of Homer from a Syriac Palimpsest.* The British Museum, 1851

Dēmaras, K. *A history of Modern Greek literature*, SUNY Press, 1972

Doederlein, L. *Döderlein's hand-book of Latin synonymes,* W.F. Draper, 1859

Eustathius. *Eustathii, archiepiscopi thessalonicensis commentarii ad Homeri Iliade*m, Volumes 1-2. , Gottfried Stallbaum, J.A.G. Weigel, 1827

Eustathius. *Eustathii Commentarii Ad Homeri Iliadem*, Cambridge University Press, 2010. This is a re-edition of Johann Stallbaum

(1793-1861) publication of Eustathii Commentarii ad Homeri Iliadem (1827-1830).

Fowler, R. L. *The Cambridge companion to Homer,* Cambridge University Press, 2004

François, R., Brunck, P. *Analecta poetarum graecorum,* Volume 2, 1785

Grenfell B. P., Hunt, A. S. The Oxyrhynchus Papyri, VI London: Egypt Exploration Fund, 1908

Gillespie, S., Hopkins, D. *The Oxford History of Literary Translation in English: 1660-1790*, Oxford University Press, 2005

Heinrich J., J. Duentzer, Zenodotus (of Ephesus.). *De Zenodoti studiis Homericis.* Oxford University, 1848

Herodotus, with an English translation by A. D. Godley. Cambridge. Harvard University Press. 1920.

Homer. *Homeri Opera.* Ed. D. B. Monro and T. W. Allen. Vols. I and II. Oxford Classical Texts. London, 1920

Homer. *Homeri Ilias.* Annotationes scripsit atque ed. S. Clarke. Ed, 1824

Homerus, Sébastien Châteillon, Plutarchus Chaeronensis. *Homeri Opera graeco-latina...,* per Nicolaum Brylingerum, ... Basileae 1561

Jebb, R.C., *Introduction to the Iliad and the Odyssey,* London, 1894.

Johnson, S., *The works of the English poets, from Chaucer to Cowper.* J. Johnson, 1810

Kirk, G. S. *The Iliad*, Cambridge University Press, 1995

Loukanēs, N. *Homērou Ilias metavlētheisa palai eis koinēn glōssam para Nik. Loukanou*, Typ. A. Ktena kai S. Oikonomou, 1870

Lucretius. *De Rerum Natura*, Oxford University Press 1947.

Macpherson, J. *The Iliad of Homer*, London, 1773.

Martial. *M. Valerii Martialis Epigrammaton libri;* recognovit W. Heraeus. Martial. Wilhelm Heraeus. Jacobus Borovskij. Leipzig. 1925/1976.

Merry, B. *Encyclopedia of Modern Greek literature.* Greenwood Publishing Group, 2004

Morrice, J. *The Iliad of Homer*, Printed for John White by Richard Taylor, 1809

Murray, A. T. *Homer, The Iliad*, Volume 1, London Heinemann, 1925

Matranga, P. *Anecdota graeca e mss. bibliothecis Vaticana, Angelica, Barberiniana, Vallicelliana, Medicea, Vindobonensi deprompta,* Volumes 1-2, typis C.A. Bertinelli, 1850

Matranga, P. *Anecdota graeca e mss. bibliothecis Vaticana Angelica Barberiniana Vallicelliana Medicea Vindobonensi deprompta.* typis C.A. Bertinelli, 1850

Morell, T. *Thesaurus Græcæ Poeseōs; Sive, Lexicon Græco-Prosodiacum*, Pote, 1762

Morello, T., Maltby, E. *Lexicon Graeco-prosodiacum.* T. Cadell, 1815

Musurus, M. Etymologicum Magnum Graecum [Greek]. Edited by Marcus Musurus. Add: Iohannes Gregoropoulos. Venice: Zacharias Callierges for Nicolaus Blastus and Anna Notaras, 1499.

Plato, *Quae supersunt opera*, Volume 3, *Platonis De Legibus,* Lib

IX, *1823,* p. 282

Pope, A., *Works of Alexander Pope*: Includes an Essay on Criticism, an Essay on Man, the Rape of the Lock, Moral Essays, Poetical Works (in 2 Volumes) and the Iliad, the Odyssey and Memoir of Fr. Vincent de Paul (as Translator).
MobileReference, 2009)

Reynolds L. D. and N.G. Wilson, *Scribes and Scholars*, 3rd ed., 1991

Scot, A., Clenardus. *Universa grammatica Graeca: Institutiones Etymologicae ex N. Clenardo...*, Hugo a Porta, 1594

Taylor, I. *History of the transmission of ancient books to modern times*. Printed for B. J. Holdsworth, 1827

Sturz, F. W. *Etymologicvm graecae lingvae Gvdianvm et alia grammaticorvm scripta e codicibvs manvscriptis nvne primvm edita*, apvd J. A. G. Weigel, 1818

Sturz, F. W. Sylburg, F., Orion (of Thebes.), Etymologicon magnum: sev Magnum grammaticae penu: in quo et originum ... I.A.G. Weigel, 1816

Schrevelius, C., Gulielmi Bowyer, G., Browne, T., Entick, J., Hill, J. *Cornelii Schrevelii Lexicon Manuale Graeco-Latinum et Latino-Graecum...* J. Johnson, 1805

Taplin, O. *Literature in the Greek and Roman World: A New Perspective*. Oxford University Press, 2000

Tzetzae, I. *Antehomerica Homerica et Posthomerica*, Fridericus Iacobs, Lipsiae, 1793

ADDENDUM: NOTES ON VOCABULARY

Details on meaning and etymology of key terms, which have presented problems to translators.

In the following accents and aspirates may be simplified or missing.

μῆνιν

μῆνιν, παρά την οργήν και την μανίαν. Η επίμονος οργή, "μηνις μεν εστίν η επιμένουσα αει και μη μειούμενη, οργή" Μηνίω
ἐπιμένουσα ὀργή, ἐκ τοῦ μένειν, οὐμὴν ἐκ τοῦ μαίνεσθαι.

Μηνις, εστι παρά την εμμένουσαν οργήν, μένις και κατ΄ επέκτασιν του ε εις η μηνις. εστι δε και παρά την μανιαν.

Μήνις, μάνις τις εστι, παρά την οργήν και την μανίαν. διαφέρει δε μηνις χόλου και οργης.
Μηνιν, παρά το μηνιω
η παρά το μένω η επίμονος οργή. κότος και μήνις
Μήνις, παρά το μένω, το επιμένω, η εναπομένουσα οργή

κότος, η οργή, παρά το κέω, κω,
η εναπομένουσα οργή κότος λέγεται

οὐλομένην
οὐλόμενος
οὐλόμενος 1 aor2 mid. part. of ὄλλυμι, used as adjective.
I. destructive, baneful, Lat. fatalis, Hom., Hes., etc.
II. unhappy, undone, lost, Lat. perditus, Aesch., Eur.

παρά τω όλλω, τω φθείρω

Ουλομένην, από του ολώ, ολέσω, ολουμένη, και εν
υπερβιβασμώ ουλομένην, και ουκ από του ούλο καθώς τίνες
φασί.
That causes loss, that causes one to perish. Loss as the loss of
a dear one.
Interesting: Poet N. Kavvadias writes "ταξείδι του χαμού".
associated with perishing, hence accursed.
ruined, lost: hence, unhappy, wretched.
"ἵετε δάκρυ καναχὲς ὀλόμενον ὀλομένῳ δεσπότᾳ" A.Ch.152;
"ἃ πλείστους ἔκανεν Ἑλλάνων δορὶ παρὰ ποταμὸν
ὀλομένους"

ουλομένην, την ολέσασαν η την ολεθρίαν. *Scholia Graeca in
Homeri Iliadem ex codicibus aucta et emendata.* edidit
Gulielmus Dindorfius. Published 1875 by E Typographeo
Clarendoniano in Oxonii.

... παράνους Ἑλένα μία τὰς πολλάς, τάς πάνυ πολλὰς ψυχὰς
ὀλέσασ᾽ ὑπὸ Τροίᾳ. νῦν δὲ τελέαν πολύμναστον ἐπηνθίσω.
Aeschylus, Agamemnon.

ἰφθίμους
ἴφθιμος=strong, stout; of rivers, of bulls, of shoulders, of souls
of men, of heads of men.

από τό ἴφθις
from ἴφι = ισχυρώς, γενναίως, strongly, bravely.

Probable etymology from ἶφι, ἴφιος

ἶφι ἀνάσσειν=strongly governing, governing with power,
Τενέδοιό τε ἶφι ἀνάσσεις (Il. 1.38) ἶφι μάχεσθαι=strongly,
bravely fighting, (Il. 1.151)

άλγεα
Ἄλγος, λύπη, πόνος

προΐαψεν
These notes support the proposition that *προΐαψεν* does not mean simply send or send forward or send prematurely *(ante tempo)*; a better translation would have conveyed the idea of sending with damage. *προ-* simply adds emphasis. A further intriguing proposition, a characteristic of good poetry, is that *προΐαψεν* was intended to convey all of these meanings: send forward, send forward forcefully, send forward in a harmful, forceful way, send forward prematurely.

προιάπτω
to send forward, to send untimely
The προ- is merely for emphasis (*Opera omnia ex recensione et cvm notis Samvelis Clarkii*: By Homer, Samuel Clarke).

Eustathius poses the argument that *προΐαψεν* does not indicate simply sending or sending forth but it indicates damage, "φθοράν καί βλάβην", because it comes from ἵπτω.
'ιπτω, ρήμα πρωτότυπον τοῦ ιάπτω καῖ τοῦ ιπόω, ο δηλοῖ τό βλάπτω. cf. Πολυδίψιον. Πολυίψιον=πολυβλαβές

ιάπτω, το βλάπτω, εκ του ιός, ο σημαίνει βέλος
ιάπτω, εις το προίαψεν

ιάπτη, διαφθείρει, καταδαπανά. παρά τον ιόν, όθεν και "αιδι προίαψεν".
(Anecdota græca e codd. manuscriptis Bibliothecæ regiæ parisiensis. Bibliothèque nationale (France), e Typographeo academico, 1841)

Other references generating images of souls sent to Hades: ψυχὰς εἰς Ἅιδην κατάγει (*The Greek Anthology*, with an English Translation by W. R. Paton. London. William

Heinemann Ltd. 1915)

τὰς ψυχὰς καταγνύουσι
κατ-άγνυ_μι, inf. -ύναι καταγνύω=break up into pieces
weaken, enervate, "πατρίδα θ᾽, ἣν αὔξειν Χρεὼν καὶ μὴ
κατᾶξαι" E.Supp.508; "τὰς ψυχὰς καταγνύουσι" X.Oec.6.5:
κατάγνυμη=break to pieces, shatter.

Xen. Ec. 6.5 τα σώματα καταλυμαίνεσθαι δοκοῦσι, και τὰς
ψυχὰς καταγνύουσι

ἐλώρια
ἔλωρ, ἔλωρα, ἐλώρια
ελλώρια Pal

The following notes support the proposition that ἐλώρια does
not mean simply 'prey'; a better translation would have to
convey the idea of torn bodies.

"ἐλώρια κυνων εγίνοντο"
Wilhelm Dindorf, Ernst Maass, Homer - Scholia Graeca in
Homeri Iliadem: ex codicibus aucta et emendata - Volume 3,
1877, p. 15

ἐλώρια, ελκύσματα. *Apollonii Sophistae Lexicon Homericum
Apollonius le Sophiste*, Immanuel Bekker, G. Reimer, 1833

ἐλώρια = ελκύσματα, σπαράγματα
ελωρ, παρά το έλω
Anecdota graeca e mss. bibliothecis Vaticana Angelica
Barberiniana Vallicelliana Medicea Vindobonensi deprompta.
typis C.A. Bertinelli, 1850

ἔλωρ, παρά το έλω, ως παρά το πέλω *Scholia Graeca in
Homeri Iliadem: ex codicibus aucta et emendata* (1875)

ἕλω=capiam
τό ἕλωρ =captura (plural τά ἕλωρα)

ἕλκω=traho
traho=σύρω, σπάω, ἕλκω

ἕλκω, το σύρω, εκ του ολκός

κυνῶν μέλπηθρα γένοιτο IL.13.233
to be torn in pieces by dogs

Μέλπηθρα, ελκύσματα, παίγνια

ἐλκέω, drag about, tear asunder
"νέκυν . . εἴλκεον ἀμφότεροι" IL.17.395
κύνες ἑλκήσουσιν IL.17.558;

"σὲ μὲν κύνες ἠδ' οἰωνοὶ ἑλκήσουσ' ἀϊκῶς IL.22.335-336

ἑλκομένας τε νυοὺς ὀλοῆς ὑπὸ χερσὶν Ἀχαιῶν. Hom. Il. 22.65

Λητὼ γὰρ ἤλκησε he did violence to Leto, Od.11.580;
"ἑ. τινὰ πέπλοιο" Arat.638:
υἷάς τ' ὀλλυμένους ἑλκηθείσας τε θύγατρας IL.22.62

"ὅταν δε [Homer] λέγη " θωων παρδαλίων τε λύκων τ' ἠϊα
πέλονται" (Il. 24.103), καταχρώμενος λέγει αντί τοῦ ἑλώρια"
Scholia antiqua in Homeri Odysseam:
maximam partem e codicibus ambrosianis ab Angelo Maio
prolata, nunc e codice Palatino et aliunde auctius et
emendatius edita a Philippo Buttmanno. Angelo Mai, Philipp
Buttmann, in libraria Myliana, 1821

"μὴ θήρεσσιν ἕλωρ καὶ κύρμα γένωμαι."
Homer distinguishes between κύρμα and ἕλωρ in other places

too.

κύρμα, what I hit by chance, prey

"κάλλιπεν οἰωνοῖσιν ἕλωρ καὶ κύρμα γενέσθαι, Od.3.271

"ἀνδράσι δυσμενέεσσιν ἕλωρ καὶ κύρμα γένησθε" Il.5.488

"Πριαμίδη, μὴ δή με ἕλωρ Δαναοῖσιν ἐάσῃς κεῖσθαι", Hom. Il. 5.684

Biographical

Michael Nikoletseas was born in Greece in 1943. After graduating from the classics section of the Gymnasium of Calamata, he went to the USA where he completed his college, doctoral and postdoctoral studies. He taught Medicine and Psychology in American universities. He is the author of books in medicine, mathematics, and neuroscience. Some of his literary works are:

Dirfyan Elegy (2010)
Far Pitched Tents (2011)
Rape in Ahmetaga (2011)
The Iliad: The Male Totem (2013)

His work has been translated into French, Spanish, Greek, and Hebrew.

THE ILIAD-TWENTY CENTURIES OF TRANSLATION

Printed in Great Britain
by Amazon